TEACHING KIDS GOOD MONEY HABITS

DISCOVER 7 WAYS TO RAISE FINANCIALLY SMART CHILDREN TODAY FOR A RICHER TOMORROW

FINANCIAL SERIES

MARIO A. VASQUEZ

CONTENTS

INTRODUCTION

"If you don't teach your children what to do with their money, marketing and advertising will gladly show them how to spend it" –Linsey Mills (Reader's Digest Editors, 2022)

The above quote by the popular children's finance author Linsey Mills rings true more than ever today. Thanks to technology, more and more marketing techniques and methods are being applied that we, and our children, are exposed to without even realizing it. In this materialistic and capitalist world, there are ads everywhere we look. Nowadays, we not only have it when walking down the street past billboards or watching TV during breaks; we have it on our phones, tablets, computers and in-home smart devices like Alexa or Google Home. The major difference is that we were only exposed to ads as kids if we watched TV, which was for a small amount of time during the day. Today our children have access to smartphones, tablets and computers at an early age and are bombarded with advertising constantly throughout their days. This has made our job as parents a lot more complicated when it comes to financially educating our children.

Many parents didn't receive proper financial education and had to learn the hard way. You probably had minimal financial education in school and didn't get that education from your parents either. While technology came along and made our job a little more complicated, it also allowed us to educate ourselves in many other subjects, including finance. As a result, we now have the opportunity to do better and teach our kids about creating good financial habits from an early age.

Because of that insufficiency of financial education in our youth, even if some of us managed to get by, we are still drowning in debt and struggling to manage our money overall as a society. So, while this book aims to teach our children how to develop good money-saving habits, many parents will also learn something.

There are a few significant points that I'm going to go through in this book, such as embracing delayed gratification, how to instill positive money beliefs in our children, how to find creative ideas to start making money early, how to avoid the pitfalls of bad debt and the importance of creating one's own business at an early age.

LET'S GET STARTED

"Rule No. 1: Never lose money. Rule No. 2: Never forget rule No. 1." –Warren Buffet (Loiacono, 2021)

The above quote was made by one of the most successful investors in the world, Warren Buffett, and it's a great quote to live by since it encapsulates how successful investors think and how we can create a mindset around that concept. This boils down to good money habits, and to teach these to your kids, we need to start from the very beginning and tell them what exactly money is. They might be old enough to have a vague idea, but it's crucial that they fully understand what it is to have a better relationship with it in the future.

Money is one of those concepts that can appear simple and

complex at the same time, but for the sake of simplicity, money is a medium that we use to exchange things, such as services and goods. As a parent, you should start talking about money with your kids as soon as they begin to understand more advanced concepts. You can also explain to them that they can see money as a tool to trade things, but money can also be saved, allowing them to buy more things later. Obviously, this is only a portion of the concept of what money is, but it's a great start. Then, give them examples of what you can purchase with or exchange for money.

As you explain what money is, you can introduce the many forms of money they will find, some of which they may already be familiar with. We are talking about credit cards, debit cards, Apple Pay, Google Pay, Venmo, PayPal and CashApp, to name a few. While these are not necessarily cash or money, they are methods we use to exchange products and services without physical currency, such as coins and notes. In other words, these are simply payment methods. To give your kids a little introduction to money, you can tell them how people used to exchange products before money existed. The most rudimentary form of exchange was called barter, which is when people exchanged a good for another good. Later, they used many different things, such as stones, shells, silver, or gold, instead of coins and bills.

There are several types of currency in the world because almost every country creates its own money used in that respective country. In the US, for instance, the US Department of Treasury (a government department) is in charge of printing money.

If the question arises, since it's a common misconception, banks do not create money; they simply offer their services to store and allow the circulation of money.

THE VALUE OF MONEY

It takes a lot of work for children to fully understand the concept of money. For example, they know that if they want to get something from a shop or store, money has to be exchanged for whatever they want. The main issue with financial literacy is that the education system (in this case, education in the US) doesn't implement it in any curriculum as a subject, like math or science. Instead, the school system introduces money, so children learn a little about the different denominations, but the teachings only go so far. It should be a yearly subject from elementary school through college. Today, the bulk of the responsibility falls on the parents and guardians to make children understand the value of money.

As adults, we know money's importance, even if we could better manage our money. Our goal is to maintain our income at a stable level and be able to purchase and pay for everything we need. However, it is also crucial that we start introducing the concept of monetary value into our children's minds. The younger you do this, the easier it will be for them. Doing so will lay great foundations for them to become more financially literate in the future.

You might have children in different age groups, and using the same approach is not exactly ideal. For instance, preschoolers need to learn something less complex, such as how much each coin is worth, while middle schoolers might be learning what savings are and how to go about them. Therefore, we will separate the approaches to money according to group age to make it easier for you to explain different concepts.

Let's start with how to talk to a child who is around preschool age. Again, as soon as they begin understanding some concepts, it's the right time to speak to them about money, its value, and what it represents. At this stage, simply showing your child what the different kinds of money look like is a great start. Nowadays, fewer and fewer children are seeing physical currency since we are slowly changing to more digital ways of payment. Showing them the various coins and bills is essential so that they become acquainted with them and can tell the difference. Once they understand which ones are which, you should get a clear glass or plastic jar so they can start growing their money (make sure it is clear so they can physically see their money increase). Teach them how to use it and show them how to count it. If you don't already have one, you should get them a toy cash register with fake money so they can become more familiar with the different denominations, and this is a great way to teach them to add money.

Another important thing you need to talk to them about is that everything we get from the store, like food and clothes, must be paid for with money. At this point, when shopping, try to pay with cash so they get familiar with exchanging money for products. Seeing the cash exchange makes it easier for children to understand the value of money instead of seeing you use a credit card or payment app.

If your child is in middle school, you can start with a few more advanced concepts about money. Some children in elementary school might be ready for this as well; you will have to be the judge of this for your children. At this stage, you're getting closer to teaching them the actual value of money, but they will not fully comprehend it just yet. They will know the difference between something that costs $5 and something that costs $50, and because they understand this, now might be the best time to introduce the concept of "responsible spending." For this, you should approach it from different angles. For instance, you can start off with being grateful, the concept of contempt, what they have, and the difference between things they want and things they need. An important concept to talk about at this age is the act of giving. This is important not only to help them become financially literate but also to help them grow into good members of society. Checking out charities and letting them pick one is a great way to get your kid interested in giving and allow them to feel how good it is to donate. One last concept that might be good to introduce at this age is "opportunity cost." To show them what you mean by that, you can come up with a simple example, such as: If they want to purchase expensive shoes now, they won't have enough money to eat out with their friends later. This is a simple example, but it allows them to think about what they prioritize more and decide which expense is more worthwhile. My children are in elementary school, and I have started explaining opportunity costs to them. They have yet to understand it fully but are beginning to, and I can see them making better decisions due to introducing this concept.

If your child is already a teenager and you've been teaching them all the basics of the value of money, then it's time to start teaching them real lessons. Remind them that contentment is an integral part of becoming financially stable, especially at that age when they tend to compare everything they have with their peers. They have to have the latest iPhone, trendy clothes, etc. But if we teach our kids to be content with what they have, they will be happier and waste less money trying to keep up with their friends. Contempt starts from within, and comparing their things to other people's things will steal their joy. It's important to remind them of this often because it's applicable at that age and throughout their lives.

Another thing that you should be doing is starting to integrate your teenage son or daughter into your household finance conversations. In the near future, they will have to be able to make financial decisions for themselves, so inviting them to listen and discuss household finances will do them well. It's common for children to hear their parents argue over their household finances since studies found money is the number one reason why couples argue, but it shouldn't be that way. If you debate money in your household, you must agree to stop arguing with your partner first. Then, integrate your teenage children into the conversation and give them a chance to come up with a solution or just get used to the types of issues that might arise. Having them present for these discussions is a great way to start financial conversations with them.

At this point, you can give them access to their bank account so they can start managing their money. If you still need to open a bank account for your child, then now is the time. Help them understand how they should be making money. In the house, you can give them more chores or allow them to get a part-time job. Whatever it is, you should be able to let them pursue some ways to make money at this age. Also, tell them about budgeting and creating a simple budget to manage their money. Explain how debit and credit cards work as you open or give them access to their bank account. They might more or less understand how they work, but they need to understand fully. This is important because credit card companies will start focusing their products on them as they grow up and go to college. If they start using credit cards before fully understanding how they work, they might get into a lot of debt.

Talk to them about the dangers of increasing debt, how interest rates work, and how they should avoid large debts and pay them in full every month. While explaining all these concepts, a great way to enhance it and help them remember this later is to give them real-life stories, even from your own life. Remember, the reason for doing this is to ensure your children acquire good financial habits and start developing them early.

HOW TO GET THEM STARTED

I've already mentioned a few ways for you to get started teaching your kids about money. This is something that they will have to deal with once they reach adulthood, but in order to engage them, you will have to come up with great strategies. Regardless of your child's age, they will lose interest quickly if you don't make it interesting.

As I've said before, starting young will make everything much easier for you and for them later in life. Their early experiences with money will shape how they behave with it once they reach adulthood. However, it would help if you made it fun, especially for young children. There are plenty of online resources where you can take inspiration. Role-playing is a great way to get them excited about money. You can devise a cashier-type game where you can purchase something from them, and they must give you the change back. Monopoly is also an excellent way for kids to learn about money, and Monopoly Junior is recommended for kids as young as five. If you don't have Monopoly or if they are under five, then you can come up with your own version of the game. There are also applications you can download, such as Amazing Coin, where kids learn the different types of coins and bills, as well as lessons on the value of money. Whatever you do, as long as you make it enjoyable, they will pay attention.

As I've mentioned, going to the store with them is a real-life experience for them to interact with money and fully understand its value. It is rewarding to allow them to purchase something themselves and give money to the cashier. If you don't deal with cash anymore, then explain how transactions are made with a card (even if it's contactless) and how the card is connected to your bank account. Explain to them why different products have different prices and what factors influence those prices. Here, pointing out some deals the grocery store is offering is also helpful. Explain how these work (whether it's a "buy one, get one free" deal or simply a discount) and encourage them to try to determine if it's a good deal based on the value of the products. This will also make them aware of when they might be paying too much for something.

If your child has pocket money, taking them to thrift shops is a great way to practice seeing how money can be used to purchase items. But it's also good to give them the idea that giving to others is an excellent way to pursue happiness. Items in thrift shops are cheaper than purchasing them new, which can open a discussion about the value of the money. Plus, teaching them to support good causes from an early age increases their chances of doing it when they are older. Buying secondhand positively affects the environment, which you should tell them about. However, none of this will mean anything to them if you're not a great financial example for them. Children are very keen on mimicking their parents' or siblings' behavior, so you should pay close attention to your financial behavior around them. Examples of behaviors they will notice are if you check what products are cheaper in the store, if you buy secondhand products or if you're always looking for good deals.

With my daughters, our favorite finance or money-related games and activities to date are; Monopoly Junior, The Game of Life, role-playing with a pretend store with prices on their toys and checking out at the toy register, shopping at second-hand stores, Amazing Coin app, SplashLearn app and counting physical money (both coins and paper money).

AVOID MAKING CERTAIN MISTAKES

We, as parents, make many mistakes when trying to teach our kids. Most of them stem from a fear of our kids doing the opposite of what we are trying to teach them. We should be doing the opposite and talking about those mistakes so that they are aware of them and can become more financially literate. Inevitable errors that we make or that parents are prone to making are what we will discuss in this section.

Many parents avoid speaking about certain subjects altogether —in this case, individual finances or the general economy—but there are many other subjects that we parents believe are taboo and should not be spoken about. This is a mistake because eventually, kids will face these subjects, whether as children or later in life, and the issue comes when they encounter them later in life and don't know how to deal with them. After all, no one has ever spoken to them about it. Nowadays, kids are exposed to many more things than we were. They acquire a tablet, a phone or other device giving them access to the internet at an early age, and they are constantly bombarded with ads for the most varied products. If we don't discuss these things, those companies' advertisements certainly will. However, when exposed to those ads with no prior exposure, they are more likely to fall for marketing tricks and will end up spending unnecessary money.

Aside from the fact that many parents avoid discussing specific topics, many believe that discussing them is pointless because their children will learn them independently. Their kids very well might, but probably only after they've made a mistake— sometimes a costly one. I am not saying that kids shouldn't make mistakes; they should and they will; it's part of learning, but if we can guide them and steer them away from inevitable errors, we should. Another issue with this method of "they will learn on their own" is that they will not be able to form good money habits early. They will likely cultivate bad money habits that are difficult to break once they grow up. They should figure out money management at a young age to bring those habits with them as they grow.

Underestimating the things they can understand is a way to protect them from the things we want to avoid discussing. Children are much more clever than we believe, so telling them about the foundations of saving and spending can be done from a young age. As long as they can understand words and basic concepts like money, we can speak to them about many other things revolving around the world of finance. Things like investing should be brought up more often in conversation because they might start to understand the basic concept of it. Of course, we don't expect them to start investing, but being familiar with such concepts will help them understand them fully when they grow up. Saving should be something that we teach them from an early age; however, what many parents tend to do is essentially force them to start saving. However, at such a young age, we shouldn't be forcing them to do anything, as they might develop an aversion to it in the future. Because we know the concept of saving and how it can help them in the future, we tend to force this habit on them. But, as you know by now, forcing or telling kids to do things usually doesn't work the way we intend. We will talk about many other ways in this book to convince them to save and create good habits without having to force them.

Giving your kids an allowance is a great way to teach them about the value of money. However, some parents believe that providing an allowance to their children will make them buy things they don't need, and it's all a waste of money. They couldn't be more wrong. Kids will learn to manage their money at a young age, but this allowance shouldn't be linked to any extra work. They should have their own allowance, and if they want to earn more money, they can do so by doing extra chores around the house. But it would help if you gave them an allowance according to their needs. Giving them too much money will make them not appreciate it, and they might spend it carelessly. Initially, give them just enough for what they need, such as buying lunch at school or allowing them to go out with friends once a week. A suitable method is to give them an allowance based on their age. But you have to be the one who finds a good balance because the cost of things changes depending on where you live.

GOAL SETTING

Goal setting is a fantastic way to teach our kids good money habits. Different-aged children will have different ways of understanding that, and we must make the right approach according to their age.

This might be something that children have never faced, so we need to navigate this carefully. There are certain steps to achieve this and get used to it. First, you need to give them realistic goals according to their age. If they are too young, you cannot set a challenging goal for them to achieve as their first goal. They will likely start hating goal setting. They should also be receptive to the goal and want to achieve it, so make those goals fun. Regardless of the age (we will go through the different methods for different ages later), there are a few steps that you need to follow. The first step is to identify the goal. This is not only something you are solely in charge of; you need their opinion and discuss this with them to understand if they are genuinely motivated to reach that goal. Consider their abilities and build the goal around them. Then, you will have to establish a time frame to complete the goal. Make the time frame realistic and achievable because a positive experience at a young age will make them want to set more goals.

Help them go through the necessary steps to achieve that goal. It will be hard for them at the beginning to plan the steps, but you must help them plan them first. You can incentivize them to write down the steps or draw a plan to reach the goal. Once they are done, you have to put each step into practice. This way, you and your child can track the progress toward the goal, which will help them stay on course. It's also essential that you celebrate when each goal is achieved. You can hang the goals on your fridge, for example, so that they can see them daily. This will motivate your kids to continue to set goals and achieve them.

GOAL SETTING ACCORDING TO AGE

Until the age of two, goal-setting has to be easy for them to achieve and gain confidence in. At this point, you might be teaching them about the different coins and bills and their different values. So, setting a goal where they know the other coins and bills by color, size, or name is a good goal to start with. Counting the number of coins and bills is also a good goal (not the value of each). Alternatively, you can exchange money for items to teach them the basics of transactions, but you should do this by the number of coins and bills rather than by their value. For instance, give them an apple for three coins instead of one dollar.

Between the ages of three and five, they are able to do more. For instance, they can now start putting money in their piggy bank or helping you do transactions in a store. They can start doing small chores for money, too, which can be a way for them to start earning money. My children recently were in this age group. They loved helping with shopping by checking prices and paying at the register.

Between the ages of five and ten, they should already know the value of each coin and bill, which allows them to make change. This is a great exercise to do at home or in a store. They can also start setting money aside for things they want so that you can create goals for those items. My daughters are currently in this age group, and they love to save for a specific toy or even just to hit a savings target of $100, for example.

Between the ages of 10 and 15, they will have the maturity to understand how money works, and you can set up a bank account for them if you still need to do so. I set up bank accounts for my daughters when they were in the three to five age range, but they didn't manage the funds. This will open many possibilities for setting different goals. You can also teach them about budgeting, so setting a goal around budgeting is an excellent practice. They can also pay for things independently, allowing them to manage their money correctly. Setting goals around how much they can save at the end of the week or month is an excellent way to establish good money habits.

Between the ages of 15 and 18, you can create a goal to save money for college, a car, or to invest. Goals at this age will revolve a lot around saving a certain amount in a certain amount of time. They can also get a part-time job, making their savings and budgeting easier to accomplish.

AVOIDABLE FINANCIAL MISTAKES

As your kid grows up and starts understanding money a little better, it's crucial that you teach them about certain financial mistakes that they shouldn't fall for once they reach adulthood. These lessons can start to be introduced around the age of eight or nine, as long as your kids have a good grasp of the value of money and how things work.

It's important to let your kids know the importance of a credit card to build up their credit score; however, we should also teach them about the negative effects of using it for everyday expenses. When using it daily, we can end up with massive debt, especially if you carry a balance and the interest rate on the card is high. This is why a budget is significant: we know we are staying within our limits and not spending money we don't have. This takes us to another avoidable financial mistake: living on borrowed money. When going through a bad economic period, asking friends, family, or even the bank for money to help us survive is common. When asking this of friends and family, there might not be any interest attached, but it might hinder the relationship we have with them. They might also need to get that money back sooner than you think, which might lead to more friction in your relationship.

The issues above may derive from a need for more budgeting or at least a reasonable budget. This is because, with a good budget, or even a budget at all, you will have control over your finances. It's important to tell your kids that without a budget, it's much harder, if not outright impossible, to reach the financial goals they have set for themselves. This might also stem from the fact that they still need to set financial goals for themselves. With goals, you have objectives that you work toward; with them, we have something to look forward to, and we will be able to become financially stable.

The absence of financial goals or budgets often leads to excessive spending. Even if they have a good salary, they might be unable to save anything. Having goals will also control the way they spend money. Maybe they won't need to eat out every day or go to Starbucks every morning. It's necessary that you calculate those expenses to show them how much money they could save per month or year and how they could use that money to work toward their goals.

GOAL SETTING ACTIVITIES

When you first introduce the concept of goal setting to your children, it might be a little hard to understand. This website's Goal Ladder activity will allow them to visualize a ladder or staircase that represents the construction of something, in this case, the steps required to reach their goals. Visualization is essential at a young age, especially when introducing concepts your kids may be unfamiliar with. Doing this activity together and talking about the steps and the respective rewards will make them understand the idea of goal setting a lot easier. This is also called "positive reinforcement," where you encourage your kid to take the next successful step.

Another great activity to set goals for kids is the "Three Stars and a Wish" webpage. Here, kids can pick up to three different things that they might want to improve on, such as "math" or "sports." They then have three stars representing their strengths and a "wish" for where they'd like to improve. It's quite didactic and easy to understand, as well as motivating.

For teenagers, you will have to introduce something a little more complex, but there are plenty of activities online for them to pursue. For example, goal-setting prompts are an excellent way for them to reach the goals they want. In this activity, they will be more encouraged to pursue their dreams because you're giving them a voice, and they have a say in these prompts. You can use goal-setting prompts to make them reach their goals for almost anything, such as saving money, budgeting, or any other topic that might not involve finance.

A vision board or a mind map are great tools to help your teenager pursue and set goals. This is something that many adults use to set goals. This is another visual-aid representation of how to choose and pursue goals. Essentially, they are creating a way to achieve their goals, whether that be through a vision board (a more creative way of dealing with it) or a mind map (a more logical way of dealing with goal setting).

At this point, you should see that it's critical to instill good financial habits in your children at a young age. Start with explaining the concept of money and what we use it for. We've already detailed several ways to do this as soon as kids start differentiating the different coins and bills. From there, we have to move on to a little more complex concept: the value of money and how parents can approach that topic without overwhelming them. I've listed many techniques for doing this, such as encouraging them to help you pay at the grocery store or letting them handle money. As parents, we sometimes make certain mistakes that might hinder their progress in terms of understanding finance because we're afraid we're going too fast. However, that is only sometimes the case. We must let them decide for themselves and stop underestimating what they can understand. That being said, we should also warn them about some avoidable financial mistakes that plague many of us as adults. It's essential to start teaching your kids the value of setting goals. This is vital to teach them at a young age because the younger they are, the better habits they will have as they grow.

In the next chapter, we will take what we've learned in this chapter and dig a little deeper. We will also discuss why we work and how money is related to that, how they can start making money so they can develop an entrepreneurial spirit, and what they can do to get started.

EARN IT

"Making money is art and working is art and good business is the best art." –Andy Warhol (Forbes, n.d.)

A ndy Warhol was an artist and filmmaker, and this quote really evokes the main subject of this chapter and is a great way to look at working to make money. Work might be a very foreign concept for a small child. Why do Mommy and Daddy have to go away every morning and only come back at the end of the day? And why don't they work on weekends? These might be questions that your children ask themselves from time to time, and it's important that, as parents, we explain what work is and why we do it. It's crucial that you shed light on the positives of work so children develop a curiosity toward it and understand the importance of it, and not instill an awful feeling, even if you don't enjoy what you do.

There are many benefits to working, such as making a contribution to society or meeting new people. It would help if you described precisely what you do for a living and why you leave the house for work. Here, it helps to explain why you have the schedule you have. This will provide your child with information that tells them that other types of work require different days and hours.

WHY DO WE WORK?

You don't want to say to your child that your work is a boring place where you're unhappy and you only go because you need money. Even if this is true for you, it doesn't mean it's true for everybody else, including your child, in their future workplace. On that note, you have to go into these conversations with a positive attitude so they have a great perspective on what work is.

The first topic of discussion is working for money. Explain that in most households, at least one parent works to earn money. This allows the family, including the children, to have a home, food to eat, and toys to play with. This is an excellent approach to start with when explaining work to a child. After that, they might want to learn more about what you do for work. Here, you will have to explain the different tasks you do throughout the day at work and explain that your employer pays you money because of these tasks. Then, when the money is received, it allows you to purchase all the different things you have in the house. At this point, they should be aware of the money exchange that happens at shops, so you can give them that as an example of how money allows you to acquire things and why you need to work.

The next thing you must go through is the benefits of work, besides the fact that it allows you to purchase items. This is because money is not the only reason we work, at least for many of us. Even if your work isn't your favorite thing to spend time doing, it has many benefits. You also interact with other people and make friends; your work might challenge you, which makes you feel good; and some work allows you to positively impact the world or improve other people's lives, for instance. You will then have to explain your schedule in detail and why it is the way it is. Nowadays, work schedules are not as linear as they once were, but it's meaningful to explain to your child why you work certain days and others you don't. If, for instance, you work in an office but not full-time, you might explain that you have agreed with the company that you'll do only the mornings so you can have the afternoons free, or vice versa. If you work from home and your work is flexible, explain that you need to work a certain number of hours a week or complete specific projects, but you don't have a fixed schedule.

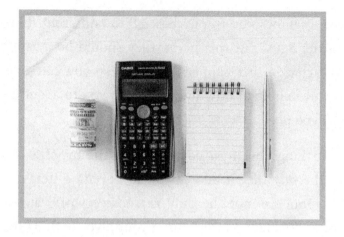

Explaining that people have different jobs will help explain why some of their friends' parents have different schedules than yours. Maybe both parents work in your household, while in the other's, only one does. This has to do with the different jobs that each one has, and the main lesson you should convey to your kids is that regardless of the time spent at home, the love a parent has for their kids is the same.

HOW CAN YOUR CHILD MAKE MONEY

Depending on the age of your child, there are many things they can start doing to earn money. If your child is under the age of seven or eight, encouraging them to do some housework is not the best approach, but once they reach that age range, they have the dexterity and ability to begin doing some housework where they can earn some money. I will divide some jobs that your kid can start doing into their age group, but ultimately it will be your and their decision to take on some of these jobs if they feel capable of doing them.

As I've said, doing chores around the house is perhaps one of the first "jobs" we can give a kid: taking the trash out, hanging clothes to dry, helping clean the yard, etc. Alternatively, ask family, friends, or neighbors if they have any small chores for your child to do.

A yard sale is a great way for kids to connect with the exchange of money, earn some money and understand a little more about the value of money. They can sell anything they don't want or no longer use in the yard sale. Kids can make the transactions if they understand the different denominations of your country's currency. Since you're having a yard sale, if your kid is good at crafts and painting, they could sell some of their work during the sale. Along these lines, a lemonade stand can also be quite a good venture for kids to get experience with work.

If your kid is a teenager, they will have more options when it comes to work. For example, if they are good at a particular subject in school, such as math, they can do some tutoring for younger children. They can also start doing some freelance work and building portfolios of things they are interested in. These are very flexible jobs that can be done around school hours, and it helps hone their skills. Many apps, such as Nextdoor, allow people to find work around their neighborhood. In this app, for instance, 13-year-olds or older can sign up for it, and the most common jobs they will see are things like mowing lawns or dog walking. Slightly older teenagers frequently get jobs at fast food restaurants, retail stores or grocery stores.

Completing online surveys is always a reasonable and easy way to earn some money, even for adults. They don't require any specialized skills and can be done during your kid's free time. If they are into social media or video games, there are a few ways they can start monetizing this interest of theirs. Influencers can earn quite a lot of money by monetizing their social media accounts. One can do all sorts of things on social media, but the first thing is to understand what type of content they want to make. Some do reviews of video games, toys, or other services; others do comedic bits just for entertainment; others can even do tutorials. If, for example, your kid loves video games and plays them all the time, apart from doing reviews on social media accounts, they can stream their games on the video game streaming platform Twitch, where they can monetize their video game abilities.

It's not all about the money, but allowing your kid to do these activities at a young age will help them develop the work ethic and the responsibility needed to have a good relationship with work and money when they grow up.

RAISING A LITTLE ENTREPRENEUR

Encouraging your kids to take on a few chores and part-time jobs at a young age will motivate them to develop an entrepreneurial mindset, which can be highly beneficial to their future. In the coming pages, we'll discuss some benefits of exposing them to entrepreneurship.

For example, exposing them to entrepreneurship at a young age can encourage their creativity. Talk to them about what an entrepreneur does—not just owning their own business but also the spirit that drives it; the spirit that allows them to look at a problem and try to fix it while moving forward. You can do this at home by exposing them to issues daily instead of trying to mask them. You can sit down with them, explain the problem at hand, and incentivize them to try and come up with a solution. It can also improve their people skills, which are extremely valuable, especially in today's digital world. With the advancement of technology, some people developed introverted abilities, which is not necessarily a bad thing, but humans are social creatures, and we need to socialize. People skills will also help them advance faster in their careers and ultimately become happier.

Something that I've already briefly mentioned is acquiring a better work ethic. This comes from experiencing work at an early age and from exposing them to entrepreneurship. In the workplace, they will see and understand what a business looks like from the inside, from the menial work of filing paperwork to interacting with others. Another thing to do to incentivize them to have better work ethics is to look at your own work ethic. Parents are the most critical people in a child's life, so seeing that you have a well-established work ethic, they will be more inclined to follow in your footsteps.

They will also develop much better goal-setting skills. We've already talked about this, but exposing them to entrepreneurship will also grow this area of their abilities. We know how kids start an activity but are unlikely to finish it and quickly move on to something else. With constant communication from the parent and seeing how entrepreneurship's end goals can create solutions, they will be more incentivized to finish whatever they've started.

Entrepreneurship is a challenging profession and often requires collaboration with other people. It's a great idea to gather some of your child's like-minded friends and present them with a problem to see if they can devise a solution collaboratively. This exercise will teach them how to work in a group and use their creativity to solve a problem. However, learning how to work together is complex, especially for children, so start with easy problems and make them more complicated from there. There are excellent puzzles and other games that will keep them entertained while helping them develop collaborative working skills. Besides that, it will also build their confidence and resilience. By finding solutions to problems, they will get more and more confident in their abilities, which in turn will make them more resilient, and they will keep thinking about a solution until they find it. Both of these characteristics will be fundamental to your child's success in life.

WHERE TO START?

If your kid is interested in entrepreneurship and wants to start a business of their own, there are many things you can do to help. Obviously, we are talking about small businesses such as lemonade stands, bake sales, yard sales, or something similar. It's not necessarily to make a lot of money but more to get them into the rhythm of being an entrepreneur and teach them the ins and outs of the industry. If it happens to make a profit, even better, but that's not the main goal you want them to achieve. Either way, you should treat this as a real business. Before anything else, you have to be able to teach them the basics of how a business works. Every business is different, but there are a few things that are the foundation of every business. Things like initial expenses and how to calculate revenue and profits are a great start.

When that's all done, then it's time to choose a business. You shouldn't be the one picking a business for them to pursue since they have to be interested in it, so let them choose what they are more interested in. If you select the business to open for them, chances are they will not be interested enough to stick with it and will get unmotivated at some point. If they don't have anything in mind, sit down with them to help brainstorm some ideas and list a few things they are interested in until they find something to pursue.

Once the business is chosen, it's time to make a plan and set goals. Since you're helping them detail this section, the first thing you should be aware of is setting achievable goals since the experiment aims to get them interested in pursuing their entrepreneurial spirit. When it comes to planning, you need to help them list everything they will need, such as materials, supplies, or equipment. Also, in the goal section, they should write down both financial goals as well as other goals they want to achieve with their business. It would help if you guided them through creating their logo and choosing a name for their business.

Now, everything is almost ready to get started. You've probably talked about money management skills with your kid at this point, but chances are that they have never practiced them. Here, we're talking about things like revenue, gross and net profit, overhead and variable expenses. Depending on your kid's age, you might have to go through a lesson with them to explain that. If you have a young child, where things like gross and net profits might still be a little complicated, you have to step in and help them calculate that. You might also have to be their investor if they don't have money saved, or at least not enough. There are numerous ways to accomplish this, including purchasing whatever supplies they require upfront or offering to do so; explain what an investor is to your child so they understand that they need to pay you back, just like you were a bank or a venture capital company. If they do not return the money to you, they are missing an essential part of the lesson related to borrowing money and repaying it to the bank or investor.

If you can, you should open a bank account for them to run the business through, or at least with both of your names, so they can see their money growing over time. To make it more realistic, income and expenses should come and go from that account so your remaining balance is the business's profit. This way, they will have a much closer experience with what it is to have a business. Depending on the type of business they start, you might have to make it legal and thus take care of the legal side of things. Some types of businesses, such as lemonade stands and other food-related companies, require a permit, so check your local city and county requirements. Others might not need any legal procedures at the start but will once the business grows and starts making more money. At some point, you might want to consider forming a company with a proper legal structure, even if you decide on a sole proprietorship. However, remember that this type of structure might put any family's assets at risk since it's not liability-free like other business structures. Consult with an attorney or a CPA firm if you need clarification on what legal structure is best for your specific situation.

If, for instance, the profits from your kids are enough for them to start paying taxes, then you will have to be the one who takes care of that, which is probably self-employment tax. However, when filling out the tax form, make sure they have a look at it so they start getting familiar with the process. One last thing: if the business fails, it's not the end of the world. Your kid might be disappointed, but you need to have them see that to accomplish important things in life, sometimes we have to fail a few times, and failure is part of life. It doesn't mean that we will never accomplish what we set out to do, but they should look at it as a way to learn from their mistakes and try again.

WHAT ARE THEY GOOD AT?

Every kid (and adult) is different, so they have different interests and skills. But when kids are too young, it's hard for them to understand and identify what they are good at, so it's your job as a parent to help them recognize what they are good at. It's easier to try and identify a kid's passion at home, where they feel more comfortable and often engage in things that interest them.

One way to do this is to introduce them to an array of different things. You can do this by enrolling them in diverse activities and sports so they can have different experiences. If you don't allow them to experience different things, they might never find what truly interests them. Encouraging them is essential, especially when trying new things; however, you should never pressure them into doing these experiments and activities, or they will simply lose interest. Instead, you should be able to incentivize them to make their own decisions and pursue what they want to pursue.

Another way to help them understand what they are good at is to engage them in DIY experiments and projects. This not only incentivizes them to pursue certain things but will also stimulate their creativity. DIY projects will cater more to their imagination and artistic side, which is paramount at that age. Things like painting, drawing, or gardening are excellent examples of DIY projects to do with your child.

While performing this array of new activities and DIY projects, it is vital that you maintain your support, and a way to do this is by asking questions so you better understand their interests. Even if your kid loses interest in a specific activity, you have to accept it and encourage them no matter what. Remember, this is their life, and it is their decision, and if they don't develop an interest in something, they will likely never be very good at it or be happy doing it.

You will soon learn about their natural interests and strengths, which is probably something they will have an interest in doing regardless. This is where you should be able to nurture their interests and encourage them to pursue them (without suffocating them, of course). You must find ways to help them develop skills related to their natural talent and promote their interest in pursuing an education related to it.

BUSINESS IDEAS FOR KIDS

We've already talked about some business ideas for kids to start, but here we will dig a little deeper and list some other business activities your kid might be interested in pursuing. You must discuss these with them and expose them to them so they can develop an interest (or not) and possibly start a business in some of these activities.

Things like setting up a lemonade stand, a bake sale, or a dog walking service are easy to create. But sometimes, your kid has no interest in any of those activities. We've already mentioned that if they are internet-savvy, it is a great idea to become an online content creator, whether reviewing video games or playing them on platforms such as Twitch or any other industry. But they might want to create things, and kids have a great imagination, so becoming inventors can be something that interests them. There are a myriad of things they can come up with depending on their interests, but this would develop certain skills such as research, design, or problem-solving.

Some kids like to entertain, whether it is by playing an instrument, doing magic tricks, or simply presenting a show. You can research your neighborhood and find out if there are other parents who would like to hire your kid to entertain during a birthday party or any other special event. This will develop their social skills, confidence, and even creativity. Other kids are very interested in babysitting other younger kids, which would help them grow their responsibility skills and time management.

Coding is something that will be around for a long time as the world becomes more and more digital. Some kids are interested in this specific area, where they learn how to create websites or apps. Many paid and free courses are available for them to learn these days, and it is one of the simplest ways to start a business.

If they'd prefer a business where they have flexibility in their hours, then making or selling things online on websites such as Etsy or Amazon can be a great entrepreneurial path to follow. This would develop their marketing or customer service skills, which can significantly help when they grow up. If they are into fashion or video games and have the ability to design costumes, then a custom maker might be the best path. The cosplay market is growing exponentially, and with the rapid increase of technologies such as 3D printing, it has never been easier to create fantastical costumes. From video games to superheroes or comic book characters, cosplay is becoming hugely popular, and there's a demand for such costumes to be made.

Your kid can start doing plenty of other things to increase their interest in the entrepreneurial area, and you will find out more about them as you discover their interests. The main lesson to take from here is to let them experience different things so they can make their own decisions.

At this point, you want to help your kid follow their entrepreneurial spirit, and as we've seen, there are many ways that you can nurture their interest. For that, making them understand the reason why we work and showing them the benefits of working besides earning money is vital. It is crucial to tell them that, because of your work, you're helping the family and other people and that your work has meaning to society. Once this is established in their minds and they get hooked on wanting to work, it's time to sit down and talk about their interests that can make money for them, even at a young age. Developing their abilities, whether teaching them better goal-setting characteristics, better work ethics, improving their people skills, or building their confidence, will help them succeed when they grow up. For that, you need to find their interests and what they are naturally good at since that will make it easier for them to carry on with the plan. Whatever they choose to follow, you should always encourage them and never pressure them to do anything they don't find interest in or will lose interest in.

When my children started to ask me why people work and what type of job I had, I found this as an opportunity to give them the "why we work" lesson. I explained not only the importance of working to earn money but also the importance of working for my own happiness. From that moment on, our money conversations have never been the same, and they fully understand what I do and why I do it.

We will leave the characteristics of entrepreneurship and making money behind in the following chapter and now focus on how they should spend their money wisely. This is very important because many adults lack the self-control to make financially thought-out decisions regarding spending money. We will talk about the concept of delayed gratification, impulse buying, tracking expenses, and creating a budget to manage money better.

SPENDING MONEY WISELY

"It's not about what we earn; it's all about how we spend what we've earned." –Stephen Magnus (George, 2020)

This quote from Stephen Magnus is an excellent indication of how important spending wisely can be to our finances. Even a person who earns a lot of money can end up poor if they don't properly manage what they've made. This chapter will tell us exactly what we can do to spend more wisely, which can be quite challenging in a world that revolves around capitalism. We will talk about important concepts that you should instill in your kids to make them aware of the importance of spending wisely.

DELAYED GRATIFICATION

This is a concept that even adults need to remember from time to time. To understand what delayed gratification is, we need to first talk about a concept that has often been present in today's world: instant gratification. This concept has been sought after, especially with the advance of technology and social media platforms. This has then trickled into our everyday activities. With instant or immediate gratification, a person seeks satisfaction right away and often without considering the long-term consequences of their choice. While seeking immediate gratification is not always bad, pursuing it at all times can have bad outcomes, such as impulsive behavior. With delayed gratification, we are withholding our desire to have satisfaction now to have greater satisfaction later.

You can test your own children to see where they stand. For instance, you can tell them they can have a piece of candy now or two pieces once they've done their homework. Whatever they decide, please give it to them. If they choose to have the candy right now, you will have to work on it and better explain the concept of delayed gratification to them. You can repeat this experience until they understand that having the candy after they've finished their homework is a better option for them; however, we will be looking at other methods too. If you're averse to giving them candy all the time, there are many other things that you can do to make them better aware of the concept of delayed gratification. For example, following the same structure, you can tell them they can have 30 minutes of playing video games now or one hour after completing their homework.

If you prefer a more money-oriented example, give them the choice of spending their allowance straight away on a small toy or saving the money to buy something else later that they would appreciate more.

Starting early with this (as pretty much everything we cover in this book) is a great way to instill the concept of delayed gratification in our kids. The environment around them extremely influences kids, so starting with an explanation stating that it's not always good to get things right away is a smart move. However, sometimes kids don't have much self-control, and we, parents, must work a little more on it.

The first thing you should do when teaching them about delayed gratification is to set a good example. If you behave appropriately regarding delayed gratification, they will be more willing to accept it. You can do many things throughout the day that can teach them that waiting is almost always a better option. But your decisions have to be a good example. Even if you think they are not listening or paying attention, that might not be the case. Kids understand a lot more than we believe, so always do the right thing when around them. When facing these decisions yourself, it's also important to discuss this with them so they are fully aware of the problem at hand.

Another thing you have to do when teaching your kid how to make decisions based on delayed gratification is to teach them how to prioritize more important things. When doing this, it's vital that you start with something small and work from there. When they make mistakes, especially at a young age, telling them off is not the best approach; instead, use the opportunity to explain what they did wrong calmly.

Teaching them about savings is an excellent way for them to understand the concept of delayed gratification. I have a whole chapter dedicated to savings later in the book, but you will have to introduce them to the topic now to make them understand the concept better. You have to make them work toward their goals, whether it is by rewarding good grades or paying them money for chores—whatever it is that will make them earn and save money. Kids can be pretty patient when working toward something they want; they might even surprise you. Help them save money with a sound plan, but also tell them to have a plan B if things don't work out with their first plan.

Even as adults, we can find it difficult to wait. So, getting distracted with something else is a great way to deal with the waiting for delayed gratification. It would help if you taught them how to create different situations when they are waiting for something to happen. There are also many techniques, such as diverting their attention away from what they are waiting for, counting backward, or making other plans.

HOW TO APPLY DELAYED GRATIFICATION WITH MONEY

The first thing that has to be done is to set goals and create a plan for achieving those goals. These goals have to be short-term as well as long-term. We can't have only long-term goals because the waiting is, well, quite long, and only having short-term goals won't allow us to achieve important things. Talk to your kid about these two types of plans and help them detail these plans and goals. You will also have to talk to them about establishing rules when trying to achieve these goals and following the plans they've made. Instead of buying candy every day with their allowance, children should do so once a week. It's also essential to track their objectives to keep them motivated and actually accomplish those goals. Sometimes it is a great idea to introduce micro-goals that are sort of milestones to those short-term and long-term goals. For example, if your kid wants to buy a new video game console in three months and they have to save $100 every month, they should check if they've achieved that $100 amount of savings at the end of each month. It's also important to guide them into setting realistic goals, or they will be disappointed when they don't reach them.

THE BENEFITS OF DELAYED GRATIFICATION

I've already mentioned some of the benefits of delayed gratification, but there are plenty more that you have to make your child aware of. When we save and resist the urge to spend money right away and get immediate gratification, we have the ability to maximize the money we earn by not buying cheaper things that we may not need but instead saving it to buy more expensive items that we will use more. For instance, we can use the example above, and you can use it with your kid. If we don't purchase candy daily, we can buy a video game console in a few months. On the other hand, if we choose immediate gratification, we might never be able to purchase a video game console.

If we apply delayed gratification, we can make the goals we've set easier and faster to achieve, which in turn will develop their money management skills. This is because your kid will understand the concept and grow up with it in their mind, which they will apply when they are older to any money decision they will face.

IMPULSE BUYING

We all know the tantrums kids like to throw when they want something. They want ice cream, new shoes, a new video game, and many more wants every time you go out shopping, regardless of where you shop. And if you don't give them what they want, then you're in for a treat that involves a lot of screaming and crying. Sound familiar?

An impulse buy is when we see something and buy it right away without thinking about the consequences that the purchase could have in the future. We, as adults, might have more or less mastered this impulse, but for kids, this is a very hard thing to overcome. It is difficult for a kid to disconnect their emotions, which makes their impulses a harder thing to control, which in turn gets them to throw tantrums when you tell them they can't have it. But the question is, "How do we teach them to halt this impulse if they don't have the maturity to fight it?"

We can do many things to help them cope with their impulse buying. The first thing to do is tell them that if they want something that you're not planning on buying for them, they should be able to purchase it with their own allowance. If they can, they will certainly do it right away. This is why you should help them create a budget. They should be able to do this with the money they get from their allowance. You will have to go through it to help them create one, of course, and this should be something that you do with them every month. To create a budget, you should take into account their own short- and long-term goals. If they want to buy candy once a week, that should go in the budget; if they want a new video game at the end of the month, that should go in the budget, as should everything else they might want to purchase as long as it's in line with their goals. This way, they will know that if they impulse buy something that isn't in the budget, they won't be able to reach some of the goals they've set for themselves.

Another fantastic method is to make a shopping list before leaving to go shopping. Going to the shopping center or the grocery store is perhaps the most challenging time for kids to control their impulse buying. This list has to be for them alone, not mixed with yours. This will also allow them to understand how much money they should take with them. If they want to purchase something else that is not on the list, they will need more money to buy everything from the shopping list they've made. A rule that many adults use that you can apply and teach your kid to follow is the "waiting period rule." This is when the kid wants something but can't buy it if the price exceeds a certain amount. Depending on the cost of the item they wish to purchase, the waiting period varies from one day to one month. So, for instance, if they want to buy new shoes on impulse, they should wait a week and see if the urge is still there. This helps when dealing with impulse buys because, with time, the inspiration dies out.

Something that works wonders is asking questions when your kid starts asking you to purchase this and that. The main goal of this exercise is to make them think critically. Ask questions such as "Do you really need this now?", "Does this need to be bought right now?" and other questions related to what they want to purchase. Spending time in the mall is something that you should m doing with your child because it can get really difficult for them to cope with their impulse buying because of all the choices they are exposed to. When it comes to shopping, don't teach them how to shop online, and avoid having your debit or credit card saved on your devices because technology has made it much easier to buy things. Shopping online is also more challenging for kids to control their buying impulses because of the constant ads that can pop up anytime.

Not letting your emotions get in the way of the decisions you should be making is important. It is hard for us parents when kids start throwing tantrums, but it's especially hard when we know they've had a bad day and want to do something nice for them. However, it would be best if you resisted the temptation to allow them to spend money that is not part of the plan, or you will be forced to pay for it. If you do that, they will expect that every time they feel bad, you are going to reward them for no reason. Essentially, you must adhere to the agreed-upon budget!

GET SMART WITH A BUDGET

Budgeting is one of the most vital tools to keep one's finances under control, and when kids have a good foundation of how a budget works early in life, they are much more likely to succeed financially later in life. When it comes to short- and long-term goals and avoiding falling into considerable debt, budgeting helps them with all of that, among many other valuable things. It will also aid them when it comes time to create a financial plan and identify financial goals. When teaching them about budgeting, it's vital that you use real-life examples to get them used to it. We will first go through some tips on how to teach them, and then we will dive into the process of actually doing it.

When teaching them about budgeting, it is necessary to consider their age. Are they ready to work with large numbers? If not, start with small numbers that they can easily add up and make calculations for. Sometimes even using the word "budget" might be a little confusing to them; when that is the case, start off with some easy examples. The example I gave when going shopping is a great one. Have them keep their allowance on them, and before going, plan what to spend so they can keep track of what they can and cannot purchase. You should be able to do that several times for them to start getting practice on how a budget works; you can also do this on birthdays, Christmas, etc. As they grow up, it's important that they know how to manage their money better and make it last longer. While the allowance they get should increase, it shouldn't be a large enough increase to allow them to stop budgeting. If they fail while budgeting one month, they can try again next month when they receive the next allowance. Again, let them fail, and don't get mad if they do so. Like everyone else, they will learn from their mistakes, but you should never cave and give them more money.

THE BUDGETING PROCESS

Once they are a little older and they've had some real-life experience doing budgets (even if you don't call them that), it's time to go through the process of doing an actual budget. The first thing to do is to calculate their income, which in their case will be their allowance. This is relatively easy to achieve since you and they know precisely what their allowance is like.

Then, you will have to identify the costs that are both fixed and variable. They should have some fixed expenses on their own at this point, such as paying for their phone, lunch, bills, and so on. These are their fixed costs and should be written down. It would help if you also told them these fixed costs correspond to rent, mortgage, transportation, or any other fixed costs adults have. Once that is completed, the rest of the money will be divided into different categories, including variable costs such as going to the movies once a week.

You need to talk to them about the differences between their needs and wants, which usually fall under variable expenses. Still, they must determine whether it's a variable expense or just spending money. Yes, their friends at school might like the new trending shoes, and they also want those shoes, but do they need them? Is that going to interfere with their already-set goals? These are the questions you should be asking.

While we will dig a little deeper into what savings are and how to save, talking to your kid about savings goals during the budgeting section is important. In this particular case, we will mention the 50/30/20 budgeting rule that helps manage budgets better, although there are many other methods for budgeting. They might want that new video game console, but that's a short-term goal. When budgeting, they should also have their long-term goals in sight. What do they want in the long run? A trip somewhere? Have enough money to pay for university tuition in advance? A car? The goal here is to find the balance between short-, medium-, and long-term goals.

It's in trying to maintain the balance that the 50/30/20 budgeting rule comes in, and it's straightforward for kids to understand since they are dividing their allowance into a precise number: 50% on needs, 30% on wants, and 20% on savings. This way, they know exactly what to do with their money. The last step in the process is to identify categories and allocate their allowance into these categories, just like the 50/30/20. But while this rule is an excellent example of how you can do this, each individual is different, and they might have different or more categories or even smaller sections inside those categories. The allocation of their allowance will depend on their goals. While with the rule above, we are allocating only 20% of their income to savings, they might want to assign more to grow their savings faster.

TRACKING EXPENSES

Tracking expenses is an integral part of creating a successful budget. There are a few things that you need to teach your kid to do so they can successfully track their expenses. First, they must figure out where to keep their money. If they're old enough to have a bank account, that's perhaps the best method, but if they're not, you and they have to devise another solution. Do they have a piggy bank or an envelope under the mattress? If they learn to save at a young age but are still unable to open their own bank account, you can open a savings account in their name so the money is safe. Smaller amounts can be kept at home in a safe place.

Regardless of where they are keeping the money, recording is an essential thing that they must get used to doing. This helps prevent them from needing to count the money every time they want to know how much they have. They can use a notebook to keep track of expenses and income and also add a date so they know precisely how their spending has been throughout the month. This is a great exercise to see their money grow, encouraging them to save more and stick to their savings routine.

Kids nowadays are tech-savvy and might find using technology to help them budget more fun. There are a few tools that they

TEACHING KIDS GOOD MONEY HABITS | 51

can use to make this happen. For instance, they can use budgeting apps. There are many different ones, and some are extremely easy to use. All they have to do is add their income and expenses as they go. Using worksheets is also a good idea if they are old enough to understand the complexities of a spreadsheet. They can use many fun templates on their computer or even their phone.

I will give you a few popular budgeting apps suitable for kids, so they can start using them. We will divide these into kids', teens', and young adults' types of apps.

For kids, you will be looking at easy-to-use budgeting applications that can do the basics of budgeting. Rooster Money, for example, is an extremely comprehensive budgeting application that comes in both a free and paid version. The free version is a simple budget app tracker, which might be enough for them to do their budgeting. At the time I'm writing this, the paid version costs $18.99 per year but has many more functionalities, such as the ability to set goals and assign chores or tasks.

Allowance+ is another great budgeting app for kids, and it also comes in two versions: one free and one with a monthly subscription. Much like Rooster Money, Allowance+ allows for the virtual tracking of funds and offers savings features. Still, if we compare the budget functionalities of these two apps, Rooster Money is better designed for budgeting.

Regarding budgeting and money apps for teenagers, there is also a wide range of options. To start with, Bankaroo is one of the best choices when it comes to budgeting apps for teenagers because it's very didactic. They can track their money virtually, see their spending, and set savings goals. However, compared to the other apps we've seen, you can assign tasks or chores with this one. While Bankaroo has an iOS and Android app, it can also be accessed through the web for convenience. There are also two versions available: free and paid at a cost of $4.99.

GoHenry is a fantastic app that not only allows teens to better manage their finances, but because it was developed in collaboration with Mastercard, it also includes many lessons on financial literacy that are appropriate for people of all ages. In fact, though I've added it to the "teens" group, this app is accessible for younger children as well. In this app, you can actually transfer real funds into it, which are protected, and because you can link the account to a Debit Mastercard, you can also use it to pay for things. When you use the card, the expenses are automatically added to the budgeting app, making it easier to keep track of everything. GoHenry also has the ability to track chores and tasks, and even though it's a paid app ($4.99 a month for one child), you can create four different accounts with its family plan option ($9.98 a month).

BusyKid is one of the most comprehensive apps on this list, covering everything from budgeting to savings and even investing. You can also link a prepaid debit card to the app so you can automatically track expenses and income in the application. The investment component is also a great addition, allowing for real investments in real stocks, so while it's very simple to use, it's best suited for teenagers or young adults who know what they're doing. Aside from that, they can assign chores and tasks as well as add allowance. While the app is free, there is a $7.99 per year fee if you want to use the prepaid Visa card.

Greenlight is a fully automated budgeting app with financial lessons and parental control features, such as notifications. The app also allows the use of a Debit Mastercard and the setting up of allowance, chores, and saving goals, and the funds are managed with real money. There's no free version of the app, which starts at a cost of $4.99 a month, but you can create up to five different accounts with the subscription.

A more complex budgeting app that can meet their needs is essential for teenagers and young adults. The apps listed below have more features and offer more flexibility, but they also allow parents to have some control over what their kids spend. One great app in this category is FamZoo. This app is fantastic if your child is starting college far away and requires a debit card. They can set up a zero-budget type of budgeting that allows them to assign every single dollar to something. This app has two versions: one is 100% virtual, while the other will enable users to link prepaid cards and work with real money. Both app versions are paid, with the digital one costing $2.50 a month while the other costs $5.00 a month.

Acorns is one of the giants of the industry, and it has been around for quite some time. It's a fairly complex app in terms of features, but it's still simple to use. With this app, teenagers can invest, budget, spend, and save seamlessly, and they also have an app that is designed for young kids called Acorns Early. It costs $5 per month, but it's money well spent because it allows you to create investment portfolios and has plenty of budgeting and savings features.

IDEAS TO SPEND LESS

Spending less is fundamental when it comes to maximizing savings, and there are many different things you can teach your kid to do to accomplish that. Spending less shouldn't only become a reality when going through a rough patch; it should be part of your everyday life.

Making product comparisons is one of the best ways to spend less money. You can teach your kid to check out the different brand products at the store and see which ones are cheaper, but they can also use comparison websites. Doing this manually can be a little more fun for kids and will help them understand how to do it. You can have a column with two or three different supermarkets or stores and rows of different products. Then, go to each store, write down the prices of each product, and compare them. Of course, this can quickly be done online too.

When shopping, doing it with a list can save your kid a lot of money.

We've already talked about this, but it's crucial to reinforce it since it's one of the best techniques to keep spending low and fight our urges to spend money unnecessarily. As long as they stay on the list, they will only spend what they should. Checking the clearance aisles for less expensive products is an excellent way to save money if one of the items on the list happens to be on sale. Still, you need to be careful because it is also an easy way to make an impulse purchase of an item not on your list with the justification that the item is on sale. Alternatively, they can use coupon websites and apps or look for coupons in the mail to help lower prices on certain things. Buying used items is also a great way to spend less. Many websites sell secondhand products, or you can check around for garage sales. Using the 24-hour rule before purchasing can also help fight the urge to spend without thinking. This is a technique that requires some training, so talking about it frequently will instill this routine in your child.

Lastly, encouraging them to use cash or prepaid debit cards is an excellent idea to keep spending under control. This way, they have a limited amount they can spend, and even if they would like to spend more, they can't.

COOKING AT HOME VS. EATING OUT

Teaching kids how to plan meals is one of the main ways to maximize savings. Not only does this keep us from eating out more often and spending more money, but by planning ahead for the meals we will make, we can save on ingredients.

It's important to teach kids how to cook healthy home meals, and soon they will start enjoying making them. I recommend planning out your meals for the week. It would help if you did this with your coupons and the grocery store's weekly flyer. This will allow you to plan meals with the items you can get on sale or with a coupon. You can try new recipes that will help broaden your culinary creativity based on the ingredients that are on sale. Also, buying store brands of these foods can be much cheaper, and the quality is almost always the same.

When it comes to vegetables, buying them fresh is a great idea, but they only stay fresh for a short time, so you will need to use them quickly. Canned and frozen vegetables are a better solution if you need a longer shelf life or more flexibility. Seasoning is relatively inexpensive and lasts for a long time, so teaching your kids to use seasoning to make their dishes more creative is a great way to eat the same ingredients but never get bored with the dishes they make.

Avoid purchasing packaged drinks and snacks because these can get quite expensive when you buy them every week. If you can't live without them, purchase them in large quantities and choose those with some versatility so you don't get bored drinking and eating the same things repeatedly. This doesn't mean you can't purchase treats once in a while. It's essential to keep your kid's motivation going, so buying desserts they like is fine if you plan everything else correctly.

My kids had this terrible habit of spending all their allowance on toys when they got the money. They often played with their new toys for a few days and completely forgot about them afterward. Once, they came to ask me to purchase a new video game console, and I told them they could do so with their own money, which, of course, they didn't have. I took this opportunity to explain to them the concept of instant gratification and sit down with them to make a plan to set goals for that video game console they wanted. It took them a few months to reach their objective, but they eventually understood both the concepts of instant and delayed gratification. From that moment on, we sat down whenever they wanted to set their goals, which they've been following religiously.

Spending wisely is one of the best ways to save and grow their money, so teaching them properly and encouraging them to create good spending habits is essential for them to use these approaches when they grow up. One of the hardest things to instill in kids is the concept of delayed gratification, but it's a fundamental one. Halting their impulse buying is necessary to keep their budget within limits and not overspend. We've gone through many different techniques that can be used to deal with this and get them into this great habit, such as having a shopping list every time they go out. Teaching them the basics of budgeting and having them start doing this with their allowance will allow them to have the capacity to budget once they enter adulthood and set short- and long-term goals, as well as achieve them successfully. There are many tools they can use to track their expenses, which is fundamental so they know exactly how much they are spending. Whether getting a notebook and writing things down by hand, using spreadsheets, or using an app, everything works as long as they keep track of their spending.

In the next chapter, we will talk about savings and the many different approaches we can use to maximize our savings. We will start with the concept of why we save, the different ways we can do it, and various methods to teach our kids how they can start saving.

AS YOU EXPLORE the pages that aim to instill strong money habits in young minds, I kindly invite you to consider leaving a brief review on Amazon. Your insights could guide other parents and caregivers toward valuable lessons for their children. Thank you for being a part of shaping a financially literate future!

SAVE IT

"Do not save what is left after spending; instead, spend what is left after saving." –Warren Buffett (Doyle, 2020)

This quote from Warren Buffett really rings true when it comes to saving, and if you're going to listen to someone's advice on finance, that would be this man. Warren Buffett is one of the most accomplished investors ever. By simply investing in reliable companies and holding them for a long time, he ultimately created one of the biggest holding companies in the world, which owns numerous companies in the most diverse industries.

Saving is the backbone of creating wealth because it allows us to accomplish many other things, including our long-term goals. However, instilling this in a kid might be challenging. So, you must start from the beginning and teach them why we need to save money.

WHY SAVE MONEY?

We adults know how much saving can help us, but kids don't, so we need to encourage them to save by giving them good reasons for it. The first thing that will teach them when they start saving is that it will help them understand the value of the dollar. They will know how much clothing or groceries cost and will understand that tracking their money is essential. Again, the earlier they start, the easier it is for saving to become a habit.

When they learn how to save, kids become more independent and self-reliant. This will also be beneficial for you because they will not rely as much on you paying for their things, or they will not have to ask you for anything they need, which gives them more freedom. Savings will allow them to stay out of debt by improving their self-control and discipline, which are easier to master if you start doing them at a young age than if you do them later in life.

By having savings, they will also be able to maintain an emergency fund, which allows them to have money for any emergency that might arise in the future. They might not be fully aware of what an emergency can do or even what it is, so you have to tell them that emergencies usually come out of the blue, such as an expensive medical bill, or they might lose their job and not have a source of income. With savings and an emergency fund, they will be able to navigate those troubled times easier.

Knowing how to save and actually doing it will also allow them to purchase things they want in the future but might not have the money for right now. This is something that they should get excited about because kids will undoubtedly want to buy something that cannot be purchased with a single allowance. Furthermore, knowing how to save can make them happier in life. While money cannot buy happiness, it certainly helps to become happier. They will not feel stressed or anxious about not having money to pay for things they want or even to help people they care for.

WAYS OF SAVING MONEY

As parents, we like to encourage our kids to start things at a young age, and saving should definitely be one of them too. We can help them become accustomed to many different things at a young age that will then carry over when they grow up and help them save money.

Most of us adults know about this, but some of us do not do it because we have never made it a habit. For example, one of the things that they can learn quickly is to turn off the water when they are not using it. Simple things such as turning the water off when brushing our teeth or even making sure the washing machine is full before we turn it on can save a lot of water. The same is true with energy: By turning lights off when we are not in the room and setting our appliances to "saving energy mode," we can save on our electric bills. A great way to teach our kids and make them do these things is by telling them that when they do them, they will be helping you spend less money on bills.

I have already mentioned how much they can save by cooking at home, and you have to teach them how to enjoy doing that. It is actually quite simple because kids enjoy doing things that they think are fun, so just make it fun. In the same line of thinking, starting to grow your own vegetables (if possible) is a great way to save money too. Most kids enjoy being outside, so if you have a small garden, taking care of your plants and seeing them grow is quite fascinating for them to see and learn how to grow their own food.

Another way to save money is to have family nights at home. There are many things that you can do at home that can be fun instead of going out to the movies or eating out. Things like board games, card games, and campouts in your backyard are all great activities to do at home that will save you money. If your kids start enjoying this more often, they will carry on this tradition when they grow up and will not need to go out of the house as often to have fun.

TEACHING KIDS TO SAVE

At this point, they understand why they should be saving and have learned a few easy ways to save around the house.

However, there is a lot more to it when it comes to saving and the different methods, as well as more challenging habits to get when trying to save.

As a parent, the main thing you must start doing is talking about it. The more you talk to them about money and saving in general, the more they retain. This is essential because, while they can retain more information than we adults, they sometimes do not retain the best information. So, constant talk is the only way to instill good information about saving.

As you know, kids nowadays are tech-savvy, which is a more fun way to learn about things. We have already gone over many apps when we talked about budgeting earlier on, and most of these same apps have saving functionalities. It would help if you used them to make your kids learn about saving quicker. Having a more interactive way to show them how to do it is a much better way to make them remember.

When they start saving, it is important that you open an excellent savings account for them where they can earn great interest. Ideally, they would have access to the app to see their money grow. Again, some of the apps we have discussed allow you to do that, but some might not be interested in those accounts. You have to find a way for them to maximize their interests with savings while also allowing them to see their money grow.

There are many stories that you can find online about savings for kids. They usually respond better to stories and retain more information if they are having fun. While there are many, stories such as "Bunny Money" or "Alexander, Who Used to Be Rich Last Sunday" are great to start with.

Talking to them about the importance of giving is crucial so they can develop those skills when they grow up. Giving is a great way to feel good about yourself and, of course, help others. However, you shouldn't have to force them to do this; instead, you should lead by example, go to charity shops and events, and explain why giving is so important.

WHERE TO KEEP MY MONEY

We've discussed this in earlier chapters, but I will reinforce the idea here once again. When it comes to places to keep your child's money, if the sum is not too large, keeping it at home might be the easiest solution. In this regard, a saving jar might be ideal. This is the easiest way to maintain their savings. Simply give them a jar large enough for them to put their coins and bills in. Another great alternative is a piggy bank, where it's harder for them to access the money once it's been placed inside. The main goal is to fill up the piggy bank with their savings until they can't add any more to it.

Moreover, a bank account is the safest place for your kid to keep the money if the sum is large enough. Ideally, you would put their money in an interest-bearing savings account where they could see their money grow over time. This is a great way to encourage them to keep saving.

SETTING SAVING GOALS

If you save without goals, you will never be able to accumulate proper savings. This is because if we don't have a goal, we cannot aim for it, and thus we cannot work toward it. This is why you must teach your kids how to set appropriate goals, short-, medium-, and long-term.

The first step is to define the type of goals they want to pursue. At first, you will have to help them understand what type of goals they want and remember that there are no wrong answers, so long as they follow through and accomplish the goals. Starting small is a great way to encourage them to pursue bigger goals.

You will also have to help them set a savings deadline because this will push them to stay on track. Without a deadline, they could get off track and back on whenever they want, but that's not the point of the exercise because when you are older and trying to save for a down payment on a house, you cannot lose track of your goals for a few months or a year and go back on track because it will simply take forever to accomplish those goals.

Nowadays, many banks allow you to create sub-accounts to add money for different goals. This will help your kid track their goals and see how far away they are from them. Some banks do not allow the creation of sub-accounts, but you can instead create different savings accounts, maybe even with different interest rates. It is important to keep the money separate for the different goals so they don't get confused. This way, it's also much easier to allocate money from their allowance and keep track of everything.

If a goal seems too daunting, the best way for kids (and adults) to reach it is to break it down into smaller portions. This is very important to transmit to kids because sometimes they want pretty expensive things, such as video game consoles, and think that their allowance will not be enough for them to get such items. In that case, they should first try to reach a third of the price, then half, and by that time, they will see they can achieve their goal.

One last important thing that will make a big difference when it comes to setting savings goals is to celebrate when they reach those goals. This will give them a feeling of accomplishment, and they will seek those feelings more often. You can reward them with an increase to their allowance, take them out to a restaurant, buy them a video game they really want, etc. Celebrating and rewarding them when they achieve a goal is an important takeaway that must be implemented.

BANKING MATTERS

Whether or not you choose to open a bank account for your kid early on in their development or later, you will have to adequately explain what a bank and a bank account are to them. This should be explained with age-appropriate words depending on their age so they can start understanding the concept.

You need to start explaining to them that a bank is just like any other business, but the services they provide are the lending and borrowing of money to people and other companies. They gather fees (interest) when lending money and pay fees when money is lent to them.

Anyone who has money in the bank has to have a bank account. The checking account is the most basic bank account that has to be open anytime you deposit money in a bank. With this account, the person can deposit, withdraw with their assigned debit card, create a credit card, and even write checks. However, these checking accounts pay no interest to the person (or very little interest) and are essentially designed to simply hold money in the account. However, there are other types of bank accounts, such as savings accounts, where the interest paid is higher.

WHY KEEP THE MONEY IN THE BANK?

There are several benefits to keeping money in the bank. While we will talk about them so you can communicate the reasons to your child, you should only create one when they have a substantial amount in their possession and when they understand how their money apps work so they can see their money grow.

The first benefit is quite simple: the safety of a bank account. While when stashing money at home, it can get lost or stolen, when keeping money in a bank account, there is none of that risk. Most banks are FDIC-insured, which means that if something happens to the money in your account, up to $250,000 will be returned to you.

It's effortless to access the money in a bank account, and with debit cards and online banking, you can access it virtually everywhere. Unlike other accounts or investments where you would need to wait to get access to your money, with a checking account, you have instant access to it, whether you want to pay via debit card or withdraw it from an ATM. The access to online banking from anywhere also allows for easy tracking of expenses, which is invaluable to staying within the budget we've set out.

Another great benefit is the fact that it is quite cheap to save money at the bank. Most of the bank's services are free, but some premium services require paid fees. However, even those are inexpensive. For instance, premium credit cards might have an annual fee, but the rewards you can get from them make it worth paying the fee. Setting up a bank account is even easy to do as well. Nowadays, you no longer have to go to the bank because you can set it up from the comfort of your home.

One of the best advantages of having a bank account is the growth opportunities it offers. Besides the savings accounts with a higher interest rate, someone with a bank account can also have access to certificates of deposit or compound interest accounts where the money grows exponentially.

There are minimal downsides to having a bank account and many benefits. Explaining this to your kid is crucial, and opening an account for them as soon as possible will allow them to get comfortable with it.

SAVINGS ACCOUNTS

As I've said, opening a bank account gives access to a savings account that allows the money in that account to grow but is just as safe as regular checking accounts. However, most savings accounts have some downsides when compared to checking accounts, like the limited number of withdrawals possible within a certain period of time, and some savings accounts are not as liquid, meaning that it might take a little longer to get access to the money.

The interest earned from the money in the savings accounts differs, so when choosing one, it is essential to check what interest they offer and other important features. Some banks like to offer promotions where the interest rate increases for a certain period of time, so researching what banks often do can also maximize your money. The rates the government announces also have an impact on the interest rates on savings accounts, which can increase or decrease according to the announcement. While most savings accounts are free, others require you to have a minimum amount in the account so they don't incur any fees.

Having a savings account at the same bank where you have a checking account is quite convenient. It is far easier to transfer money from the checking account to the savings account and vice versa, and some banks also offer better promotions. Many banks where you have a checking account will also allow you to have more than one savings account, sometimes with different features to manage your money better.

BALANCING A CHECKBOOK

Teaching kids how to balance their checking accounts might not be the most fun thing they will have to do, but it is a great way to keep things in order and avoid debts. While balancing a checkbook might seem like a thing of the past because of the rise of online banking, knowing how to do it still has its advantages (and should still be done). Checkbooks are made of paper, and the checks are used to purchase items or services. Within the checkbook is a worksheet where the person can write the transactions. Most people no longer use the paper worksheet within the checkbook, but essentially, it was a record of transactions that had to be done by hand. How exactly did people do it?

As I have already mentioned, the first step is to write down all the transactions (both money in and money out). On one of the columns labeled "Cash Balance," you would write the amount of money that was currently in the account. Then, you would write down the transactions you have made. At the time, people would do it in two different ways: they could write down the transaction as soon as they made it, or they could keep the receipts and do it later.

Then, you would have to open your checking account statement, which could come in a paper copy that comes through the mail, or you could have also gotten it through your email.

Then, you would compare the transactions on the checking account statement and check if those were the same as in the checkbook you have written down. In the event that some transactions were missing, you could add them. You can teach a version of this to your kid so they get more comfortable dealing with and managing their bank account. I still balance my checkbook every week, but I use a spreadsheet on a computer now instead of the small paper version that comes with my checks. Yes, I still even have checks to pay for some items.

After earning and developing good financial habits, knowing how to save is crucial to becoming financially successful in the future. This is one of the main components where parents should spend more time teaching their kids properly and enabling them to create a routine, as well as to check their savings regularly. Giving them the reasons why we should save is a great way to start. Then, move on to the different ways of saving throughout our day and develop the proper methods and techniques they can use to maximize their savings, which in turn will allow them to set savings goals and keep track of everything.

When they start, perhaps a piggy bank or a savings jar is enough to keep their money, but as they grow their money, opening a bank account might be better to keep their money safe and enjoy the advantages that banks offer. From there, opening a savings account is the next step, where they can actually earn more money by simply stashing their money in the account and watching it grow, which is a sure way to keep them motivated to save more!

In the next chapter, we will go through the many different ways kids can make their money work for them. This is one of the best ways to increase their savings and money in general without doing anything in particular. This is a more advanced part of the book, so make sure they fully understand what we have talked about so far so they can dive into the world of investing.

LET THEIR MONEY WORK
FOR THEM

"It's not how much money you make, but how much money you keep, how it works for you, and how many generations you keep it for." –Robert Kiyosaki (Ruth, 2015)

Robert Kiyosaki is one of the best-known authors in financial literature, as well as a businessman and entrepreneur. His book *Rich Dad, Poor Dad* is one of the most popular books for anyone trying to get their finances in order and build wealth. In fact, it's an excellent book for you and your kid (when they are a little older) to read. In this chapter, we will discuss how you can teach your kids to make their money work for them. Essentially, you will have to explain to your kids what investing is, and you have to do this in simple terms, regardless of their age. So, how can you do this?

Investing is when you put money into something, such as the stock market or buying a property, with the goal of having that money grow over time without doing anything. There are many different ways to invest money, and we will talk about some of them later in this chapter. But for the sake of a simple example, imagine you put money in the stock market, which is one of the best ways to grow money but usually carries more risk too. On average, the stock market grows at a rate of 10% in a year, but this is the average over a long period of time. So, assuming you have invested $3,000 over a period of 30 years without adding any more money, you would have around $50,000. This is because, assuming the stock market gives exact returns of 10% every year, which is unlikely since this is just an average, in the first year, the value of your stock would increase $300 (from the $3,000), in the second year it would increase another $330 (from the $3,300) and in the following year, you would have $3,993 (from the $3630). It keeps on compounding every time, so the 10% return is not only on your initial $3,000 but also on the added value earned over a year. This is why the stock market and specific compound interest investments are so attractive to investors. There isn't a minimum to start investing (although some brokers do have a minimum), but the good thing is that you can start with $50 or even less and add more as you go. I have already mentioned some apps where kids can start investing, and it is important for them to start early so they get confident in their skills and how things work, and as you have probably figured out, the earlier they start, the more time their money has to grow.

WHY IS IT IMPORTANT?

Besides the reasons I've given above, there are many other reasons why investing can be an essential practice for anyone, including kids. They will develop good saving habits, which are already on track because of the savings methods and budgeting they should already be doing. They would also learn how to take risks, not only with their finances but in life too. This allows them to calculate their risks before jumping in, which can be quite beneficial throughout their lives. Obviously, compounded returns are a great advantage since they can exponentially increase their investment without adding anything to it and just letting their money stay where it is and let it grow. Because investing is not all about returns, since it is a risky investment, sometimes we do lose money when investing, but starting early will help us recover from those losses that we might make along the way.

Also, because of the exponential growth of our investments, financial security will come way sooner than if we did not invest. This means that in 10 years if your investments have grown exponentially, you might already be financially stable.

HOW TO INVEST

Investing is a broad subject that sometimes even we parents do not fully comprehend. However, it is our duty to teach our children the best we can, starting with the basics and expanding their knowledge from there. This subject might have been outside your plans when you set out to educate your child to become financially literate, but if you want them to have the full scope of what it means to be financially knowledgeable, then investing is an essential component. Before starting to teach them about investing, they should be fully aware of the concepts we have discussed so far, such as having a solid foundation of money, savings, and spending. You will want to talk about a few things when telling them about investments, such as the way they should think about companies, how the stock market works, what the different risks of investing are, and how to start investing.

Things like asset allocation or portfolio management might be left until they have a good grasp on the basics of investing, but once they fully understand that, you can start with more complex concepts. For instance, starting off with the correlation between risk and reward is a great way to talk to them about investments. They should already have a savings account, so it will be simple for them to understand. When the money is in a savings account, the risk is low or even nonexistent because you know how much money you will have when interest arrives, and the value cannot decrease; even if the interest changes, you will be notified. While savings accounts have no risk, stocks are one of the investments with the highest risk in the financial world. This is because stocks can increase and decrease in price at any moment throughout a trading day, so if they have $100 in a stock at the end of the day, they could have $150 or $50. In this case, it would be a very volatile stock, but some can be less volatile. However, between a low-risk savings account and a high-risk stock, there are other financial instruments that have a more balanced risk-reward correlation, such as bonds. Bonds are considered low-risk, low-return types of investments but still have a higher risk than a savings account. These types of investments pay interest to the investor, and at the maturity date (when bonds expire), the investor will receive the money they have invested. There are a few types of bonds, such as those backed by the government or banks, that never default, so they are less risky, and those backed by companies, which offer higher returns, but the company can default, and the investor might lose some of the money invested.

Now, if your child is still young, all this talk might be quite hard to follow, so to keep their attention, you can't just talk and talk without any interactivity. If you own stocks, it is important that you let your kid have a look at them so they might see familiar companies there and make the connections. Another good idea to keep their attention on is to go to brands they know and check their company's page, where they can learn more about what specific companies make. Once they have a basic under-standing of how the stock market works, it is time for them to buy a share of a company. Even if they cannot have an account yet, you can let them buy one from your account (it doesn't need to be expensive, so it doesn't mess with your portfolio). The exercise is to go back to it every week and check how it's going. Once they get older, you can help them properly analyze stocks and allow them to make additional purchases. At this point, they might even have their own money so they can purchase their own stocks. If they do not have money, then you can lend them cash so they can start to get excited about owning stocks, or you can use the "practice" part of the brokerage account where they can select some stocks and have a portfolio, but it doesn't require real money.

There are many different ways for a kid to have their own brokerage account, whether through a custodial account where you are the owner of the account with a minor account associated with it, or they have their own (still opened by you). This is because when an underage child has a brokerage account, all the potential gains and taxes still have to be handled by the parent or guardian. A custodial account is in the child's name, which means that they own their assets, but you still have control over the account, such as the decision to add or withdraw money. However, when this occurs, the gains and taxes are in the name of the child, which can be advantageous for the parent in terms of taxes, and because the child usually has no income, they do not have to pay as many taxes.

WAYS TO START INVESTING

In this section, we will talk about the many different investments you can discuss with your child. It's important to start slowly and take your time to explain because, depending on the child's age, things might get confusing quickly.

STOCKS

It would be best to start with stocks since they are the most talked about of all investments, and linking a company to the stock makes it easier for your kid to understand what they are. Picking a company that they are familiar with is a great way to start, but because they still do not know how to do the due diligence on their investments, you need to help them pick a company that will stand the test of time since you want your child to have their money grow over the years. Explaining the stock's underlying businesses and what they do should also be easy for them to understand, so Microsoft, Sony, Apple, or Nintendo might be some of the companies that they will understand quickly because they are already familiar with them. Other video game companies or clothing companies are also easy for them to understand their business model.

Other than long-term investments, domestic companies can also be a great choice because you know they are well-regulated, and you (or they) will not have to pay any extra fees. Stocks that pay dividends might also be a good thing, not only because they will give your child more profits but also because they will start to understand what dividends are and how they work.

MUTUAL FUNDS

The best mutual funds for your child might not be very different from the best mutual funds for adults. You would like them to have consistent growth so that they can increase their wealth. If you search for "mutual funds for kids," you might not find exactly what you are looking for because these funds claim to have a "child plan" with goals tailored to their needs, but they don't tend to be great for the child's future growth in terms of money. Instead, you usually get an extremely safe and low-growth fund, where they might not lose any money but do not grow that much over time either. Instead, check more "normal" mutual funds so they see more significant growth over time. Now, when it comes to choosing the right mutual fund for your kid, this depends on many factors. What is their primary goal? What is their (your) appetite for risk, volatility, etc.? I will give you some examples of good mutual funds to invest in for your child based on some due diligence I have done (don't take my word for granted here; these are just examples, and even though the following mutual funds have performed well over the years, it does not mean they will continue to do so).

The Axis Blue Chip Fund is a low-risk mutual fund that has been performing well over the years. A large part of this mutual fund portfolio is focused on large-cap businesses, with some mid-caps in there too. This way, they can minimize volatility and still have some good gains. The estimated returns for this mutual fund in the next three years are 19.56%.

The SBI Small Cap Fund, as its name suggests, is focused on small-cap companies, which means it is riskier than the mutual fund mentioned above. This mutual fund has an estimated return of 15.05% over the next three years. One of my favorite long-term strategy mutual funds is retirement target-based funds. All the major companies have their own version of these types of funds. Fidelity, for example, calls theirs "Fidelity Freedom Funds," with 14 different funds to choose from. You select the fund based on the year closest to your expected retirement date.

BONDS

Bonds are safe choices when it comes to investments that also pay interest over time. In a very simplified way, bonds come in two types: governmental and company. These entities issue bonds to borrow money, at which point they then pay interest to investors, and you receive the capital spent once the borrowing is over. You can also give bonds to your child, which then stay in their name. To purchase, you can easily go to TreasuryDirect.gov, where you can add their name to the bond and make the purchase. You and your child have to have separate accounts on the Treasury website, and you will have to provide their Social Security number.

REAL ESTATE

Real estate is an excellent way to invest money, but it might be hard for kids to invest in real estate at such a young age. However, there are ways you can have your kid invest in real estate, even while they are underage. This is because real estate investing involves more than just the direct purchase of properties such as apartments or houses. Other investments, such as REITs (real estate investment trusts), can be purchased through the stock market. These are similar to mutual funds but purchased through shares. An excellent REIT example is Realty Income Corporation, sold on the New York Stock Exchange under the stock ticker "O." Besides going up in value, O has a guaranteed monthly dividend pay just like if they collected rent.

If they purchase REITs, it is quite easy for them to see their money grow because of the monthly or quarterly dividends they receive. It is also important to explain to them the business model of these types of investments, where the fund owns properties. When they buy a share, they are actually purchasing a small part of several properties.

EXCHANGE-TRADED FUNDS

Exchange-traded funds, or ETFs, are a great way to diversify a portfolio. They are identical to mutual funds or REITs in the way that they are pooled funds. Unlike mutual funds, they are traded on the stock market, and they can track many different indexes and industries. ETFs are a great way to start investing in your kid's future because they are less volatile than stocks since they have several companies within the same fund, but at the same time, they also offer some growth depending on the ETF purchased. Another great thing is that there are many different types of ETFs, such as those in clean energy, the automobile industry, technology, etc., which is great since they can choose what interests them the most.

CERTIFICATE OF DEPOSITS

Certificates of Deposit, also known as CDs, are very low-risk types of investments that are usually short-term. These are great if your kid has some money saved and wants to earn some interest on it without almost any risk. This can be a great way to teach your kid to invest their money without being exposed to high risks but still getting returns on the money invested.

They can deposit a lump sum of money for a specific amount of time, and they can only touch that money once the expiration date arrives. This is the main difference between CDs and savings accounts, where you can withdraw the money deposited. They might have to pay a penalty if they withdraw the money before the expiration date. Because of this, CDs usually have a slightly higher interest than savings accounts but are still low-risk.

HOW TO GET STARTED AS A CHILD

We've already seen some ways your underage child can start investing, but there are many others. In this section, we will look at the different accounts that you can open for your child so they can start investing.

A jointly owned brokerage account is a great way to do it. These allow for more than one person to have a different profile within the same account. As a parent, you will be the primary account holder, but your child can have their own portfolio without affecting your own. An example of such an account would be Fidelity's Youth Account.

Another option would be a custodial account, where a kid can have their own account, but the parent or guardian still manages it because it is in their name. In these types of accounts, they can invest in a large array of investments such as stocks, CDs, bonds, and more. The main change here is that any investments and withdrawals of money have to go through the parent or guardian. Acorns Early Account is an excellent example of a custodial account.

There are other accounts, such as the custodial Roth IRA, where you can help your child save for retirement. If they have some money saved, this is a great place to keep it. There are two types of IRA accounts: traditional, where the money invested is "pre-taxed," which has immediate tax benefits for those earning an income that is big enough to owe the government taxes at the end of the year. However, they will pay taxes when they eventually withdraw the money at retirement. The Roth IRA doesn't have the tax benefit right away, but this isn't a problem since children usually do not have a significant enough income to pay taxes and the big benefit is that they will not have to pay taxes when they withdraw the money.

As I have said, investing is a big part of growing wealth and being financially literate and stable. The younger your kids start investing, the more they can grow their wealth, and that is why it is so important to start talking about it and eventually encourage them to start investing. However, before that, there is a lot that you have to tell them about. For instance, they have to be aware of the risks of investing but also the "magic" of compound returns, where their money can grow exponentially. A concise explanation of all their investment options is also important so they know what to expect and how to invest in the future when they do it themselves. As we have seen, there are many ways you can get your child to start investing, from joint brokerage accounts to custodial accounts. You should choose the one that works best for them and for you. Ultimately, this is an excellent exercise for them to tip their toe in the world of investing and get excited about investing, grow their wealth, and make their money work for them.

In the next chapter, we will talk about borrowed money. This is a crucial chapter in the child's development of financial literacy skills and one that many adults tend to forget. We will focus on good and bad debt, how they can avoid falling into a big debt, and even how to get out of debt if they get into one.

BORROWING MONEY

While Josh Billings, an American humorist, did not work in finance, debt is undeniably a problem that affects everyone in any industry, and his quote is certainly accurate. Why? Well, primarily because things are structured in an easy way for people to fall into debt while making it quite hard to get out of it due to the increasing interest that starts accumulating as soon as the debt starts.

In a very simplistic view, debt is what you owe to somebody or any financial institution like a bank. This money is usually lent for a certain period of time, and you will have to pay it back, whether in one lump sum or through installments. Many financial institutions allow people to borrow money but charge interest on the money borrowed, so you will always pay more than what you originally borrowed. In fact, that is one of the many ways banks make money. From a bank's perspective, the interest rate and amount of time you have to pay that money back will depend on your credit history and how trustworthy or reliable you are in paying it back. There are many different types of debt that will change depending on your needs or creditworthiness, and while most debts are bad, there is also what is called "good debt."

Your child might have heard of debt and associated it with a negative connotation. While this is not necessarily a bad thing since most debts are bad, it's not entirely true. They can question you with points like, "Why would anyone go into debt if they had to pay back more than they received?" There are numerous legitimate reasons to take on debt, and it is frequently used to bridge the gap between a person's income and spending. Other debts are needed, such as a mortgage to pay for a house or a car.

GOOD DEBT VS. BAD DEBT

While the term "good debt" might sound like a contradiction, it's not because if someone incurs a good debt, they can increase their credit score, how much they can borrow in the future, and even negotiate better interest rates for mortgages. However, a good debt is when you can repay the money you borrowed in a timely manner so that it does not increase expo-nentially over time and become hard to handle. In the same line of thinking, a bad debt is a debt you cannot pay or cannot pay on time, which increases as time goes by. Explain to your kid that if they are incurring debt by paying for groceries, bills, or any day-to-day expenses, they are probably growing their bad debt. This often means they do not have enough money to spend on regular things and are spending more than they can afford. Borrowing money should only be done if they have to spend it on things that cost a lot of money, and it is not conve-nient to pay for everything at once, such as a new TV, a sofa, a car, or a house. However, for the first two, you might want to pay them as soon as possible because, unlike the purchase of a car or a property, a TV or a sofa will not necessarily increase your net worth. However, it might be nice to pay for them over a few months rather than dipping into your savings to pay for those things.

Some people are able to borrow large amounts of money with their credit cards, but this doesn't mean they should use all of the money available to them to do it. Furthermore, banks and other financial institutions charge high-interest rates on every dollar lent, so the more you borrow, the more interest you must repay. Since they are kids, you will probably be the primary lender if they borrow money. However, do not simply lend them money without an efficient way for them to pay you back, and especially pay you back in a timely manner. This is impor-tant because they will start to understand how debt works and how difficult it can become to repay debt if we spend sense-lessly above our means.

As I have said, there are a few different types of debt, and you must explain to your child the differences between them. The most popular type of debt is credit card debt. Your kid might be familiar with the term or even how they work. A credit card is just like a debit card, except that instead of paying things from our checking account with money that we have, we are spending money that we do not have, and it comes from money that the bank has. Explain the grace period credit cards have, which is the time between the statement closing date and the due date for the payment. You will not incur interest fees if you can pay the entire balance in full. So, if they have spent $1000 and cannot pay the total amount within the grace period, they must pay back the unpaid amount plus interest. While having a little debt on their credit card is not necessarily a bad thing (in many cases, it is a good way to build credit scores), it is the type of debt that they will want to pay off as soon as possible so it doesn't grow to a point where it becomes tough to pay back. Since credit cards typically have very high-interest rates, carrying a balance on them can cause the total amount owed to the bank to snowball out of control. This is how many people get into debt without knowing how to get out.

A mortgage debt is something that many people take on since it helps them pay for their houses. When paying for a property using a mortgage, they still have to have money to pay for the down payment, which is a percentage of the property's value. In a mortgage, the lending institution (usually a bank) also applies an interest rate, and the better their credit score, the better their interest rate. It is also important to note that the more they pay as a downpayment, the less interest they pay. If the downpayment is at least 20% of the property's purchase price, that will also help them get a lower interest rate. Another reason why mortgage debt is considered good debt is that the interest paid each year is typically tax deductible.

A personal loan differs from a credit card because the bank or the financial institution is lending a lump sum of money, and it has to be paid within a limited time frame. The way these personal loans are paid differs depending on the type of arrangement, which will also change the interest on the loan. Usually, a missed payment on a personal loan can have many more consequences than, for example, a missed payment on a credit card, which can include a lower score on their credit. Student debt is also something that many people incur due to the high cost of higher education. However, this can be seen as an investment in their future that will allow them to make more money later on. This loan is usually paid after they finish their studies, which can complicate their financial situation if they do not have a financial plan. Nevertheless, student debt is not a bad thing, and sometimes it is a necessary thing to have.

There are a few words of advice that you should give your child. For example, tell them to stay away from payday loans. These types of loans can get out of hand quite quickly. Always make sure they come up with a plan to be able to pay off their loans as fast as possible. Also, make sure you teach your kid what real interest is. Borrowed money is usually more expensive than they might think, and if you have to lend them money, make sure that you also set up a plan for them to pay you back so they get used to it.

TEACHING KIDS ABOUT DEBT

Now that your child has a better idea of the types of debt there are and the differences between good and bad debt, it is time to talk about some general knowledge about what debt represents in people's lives. As I have explained, just because a lot of people have debt does not mean that it is a good thing. Because so many people, including perhaps in their household, have or talk about debt regularly, kids might think that it is not a big deal. Having a large amount of unmanageable debt can cause a lot of stress to people, besides the inability to pay for their regular expenses. However, taking on a little debt can actually help and even put them in a better financial situation in the future. This is the case when taking on student debt to pay for higher education or taking out a mortgage to pay for a house. Even having some credit card debt is not a bad thing if it is manageable and they are trying to build or increase their credit score.

However, a debt is a debt, and they will always pay more than the borrowed amount. Debts, where the borrower does not pay any interest, are very rare, and even so, these might have fees to protect the lender. Not paying their debt on time can have devastating consequences for their financial life. In some cases, they might even have problems with the law if they do not pay their debts on time.

Before taking on debt, your kid should consider their options. Being honest when considering taking on a loan that will incur debt is vital. Encourage them to think clearly about what they are doing and ask themselves questions, such as, "Why are you taking on a loan?" Is it because they need it or because they want it? Do they need the money to purchase something now, or can they wait? Can they pay the money back on time while still paying for their daily expenses? How long is it going to take to pay the money back? These are all questions they have to ask themselves before they take on a debt, which can also save them from getting into a very difficult situation.

HELP THEM AVOID DEBT

The best way to help them avoid debt is by teaching them the consequences of debt and encouraging them to follow a few rules. Chances are that your kid will incur a debt at some point in their life, but getting out of hand with a debt is something they can avoid.

The first thing is to make sure they fully understand how credit works. We have discussed it extensively in the paragraphs above, but it is essential to reinforce this point. Other things that we have also talked about that will help avoid debt are teaching them how to save and how to budget. Planning ahead of time will also be highly beneficial to them—whether it is planning their loans, their budget, how they can repay borrowed money or anything else related to their money.

Setting limits is also crucial. They must understand that they cannot have everything they want when they want it, and some things require time and planning. Overspending and over-financing can be easy things to do, especially if there is no plan behind them, and things can get out of hand quickly. Teaching them to envision financial success is also a good thing that is better done at an early age. This also comes from having great money habits and learning about all aspects of finance early on in their life.

GETTING OUT OF DEBT

Your child now knows about earning, saving, and budgeting their money and how to spend it to not live beyond their limits. This is all great, but life can sometimes be a little more complicated, and your child might get into debt, especially if we are talking about student debt and a mortgage, but also credit card debt or personal loan debt. As parents, we do not want our kids to be in debt, so teaching them ways to get out of it faster should be a priority for us.

Ignoring a debt was undoubtedly a mistake we all made at some point when we were young, and it might be your kid's first time ignoring a problem, but they will soon understand that it will not go away that easily. When facing debt, they should first write down their list of debts, such as credit card debt, student loans, etc., and who loaned the money to them. In this list, they should also write in front of the name the minimum amount they should be paying every month to the lenders, with the interest rate added in. This might be hard to do because they

are actually realizing how much debt they have, but it is necessary to start getting out of it.

There are many ways to pay off debt faster, but three strategies
are quite popular: the avalanche method, the snowball method,
and the 50/30/20 rule. In the avalanche method, it is ideal if
they feel like their debt is too big to handle and is getting out of
hand. Here, they should try to pay the debt with the highest
interest first (note that this is not the highest debt), and once
that debt is paid in full, move on to the second highest interest
debt, etc. In this method, they should still be paying at least the
minimum monthly payments on all other debts. While using
this method, they are using a strategy that will help them pay
less overall, but it isn't necessarily the fastest method to clear
their debts.

In the snowball method, they should start with the lowest debt
amount (not the lowest interest debt) and then move on to the
following lowest debt amount. Again, they should still pay the
minimum amount on all other debts they have. This method
encourages people to continue tackling debts one by one since
clearing one debt, even if it is small, will help them get motivated. Lastly, the 50/30/20 rule is something we have already
discussed in the budgeting section, but it can be an excellent
way to get rid of debt quickly. If you remember correctly, 50%
of income should go to needs such as groceries, rent, etc., 30%
should go to wants such as going out, streaming services, and
so on, and 20% should go toward debt and savings. If they have
debt, this should be paid before the money goes to savings, and

they should only use this technique if they are not drowning in debt.

Another great way to tackle debt is to create a budget or financial plan that includes debt repayment, as I mentioned in the budget chapter of this book. Here, you should help your kid understand how much debt they might have and how much they can pay, then add that to their regular monthly expenses.

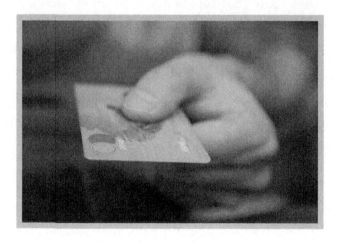

TIPS TO PAY OFF DEBT FASTER

Regardless of the method used to tackle debt, there are other things they can do to help you pay off debt faster. One of them, which I have already mentioned, involves paying more than the minimum required. If using one of the methods above, focus on paying more toward the one you are tackling first, and the others can be paid the minimum amount due each month. If you pay the minimum for the others, you will finish paying the debt you target faster. Usually, the minimum payment is only slightly higher than the interest gained every month, so they would be paying debt off for many years. They can also make lump sum payments when they can. Ideally, this should be done regularly every two or three months, but sometimes that is not possible. However, doing it when they can will help them pay off their debt quicker.

Restructuring debt can also be a possibility, but this only works for some debts. When doing this, there are many possibilities, but the most common one is changing their high-interest debt into a lower-interest debt, allowing them to pay it faster. They can also consolidate debt by putting it under one loan with one interest rate. Alternatively, enrolling in autopay is an option where they can set up money on the side immediately so they do not forget about paying off their debts and incurring extra fees. If they have the time, earning additional income will always help pay off debt faster. Whether working extra hours or during weekends, it does not matter as long as they bring in more income to pay off their debts faster.

There are other things your child can do to prevent getting into vast amounts of debt. One is something that we have also talked about, which is building an emergency fund. With an emergency fund, they can use it to pay lump sums of money every now and then and tackle debt quicker. Paying off their student loan before they start charging interest can also be a possibility, even if it might be harder to do it as a whole. However, they can start paying as much as they can so they have less debt and can pay less as soon as the interest kicks in. Taking a gap year before they start their secondary studies, where they just work, can also help them pay off their debt quicker. In this year, they would just make money and save as much of it as they can to pay off all their debts, especially their student loan debt.

Debt will be something your child will have to deal with at some point in their lives, so shying away from it and not talking about it with them will only make their life more complicated. Sometimes taking on debt is necessary so they can get a better job in the future or pay for their house; other times, it is entirely unnecessary. Knowing the difference between good and bad debt will help them identify which one they are taking on. You should tell them everything about debt before they grow up and start taking on credit card debts, and more importantly, you should teach them how to avoid debt in the first place, along with how to get out of debt as quickly as possible.

In the next and final chapter of the book, we will talk about how to build good credit and its benefits. We will continue to talk about credit cards, but this time for their benefit and how they can use them responsibly. I will also mention why it is so important to have a good credit score and what credit is in general.

BUILDING GOOD CREDIT

I mproving the credit score can be an excellent advantage for your child as they begin their adult life. It is our job to make sure they have the necessary tools to thrive and become financially stable as soon as possible. But the truth is, having a great credit score is not a trend that is happening right now in the world, in general, or in America in particular. About 18% of Americans have a credit score between 580 and 669, which is considered fair, and only 1.2% have a credit score of 850, which is a perfect credit score (Ulzheimer, 2023). Because of this, around 42% of Americans have been denied a personal loan or a credit card (Davies, 2022). This is not a great look for people who want to go on to have mortgages or need to borrow money to purchase essential items.

The first thing we need to do as parents is teach our kids about credit cards properly. We have already touched on the subject earlier, but now we will dive into it in more depth. In a straightforward way, when a credit card is used, we borrow that money from a bank or any other financial institution that has issued the credit card. This means that the money we have just used is not ours and must be repaid with added interest, assuming it is not paid off within the grace period mentioned previously. There are a few key players in how credit cards work:

- The cardholder, which is you.
- The merchant, which is the place where you use your credit card to purchase things.
- The acquirer is the bank or the financial institution that processes the transaction from the merchant.
- There is the issuer, which is another bank or financial institution that issued the credit card and is where the money is coming from.

When the credit card is used to make a purchase, the merchant sends that transaction to the acquirer. The acquirer sends that same transaction to the bank that issued the credit card, which is the institution paying for what you bought in the first place. At this point, the issuer checks the credit limit and outstanding money and approves the transaction if the cardholder still has available credit on their card. Upon approval, the acquirer gets approval for the transaction and sends it to the merchant, allowing the transaction to be completed. This way, the acquirer gets paid by the credit card issuer, and the issuer gets paid by you in the future, possibly with added interest. In this arrangement, the acquirer gets a small part of the money from the transaction, and the issuer makes a profit by charging interest to the customer.

TIPS TO USE A CREDIT CARD AND BUILD GOOD CREDIT

If you have followed all the topics until now, your child probably has a good grasp of what a credit card is and what it is used for. Besides that, having a good knowledge of how money works and its basics is also essential for the next section, which we have also covered in past chapters. After you are sure they understand the basics of money, you can mention checking accounts and even allow them to have one. Then, it is time for you to introduce credit cards and everything that involves having a credit card. I have already covered the basics, so I will not mention them again, but make sure your child understands them. By now, they must know that a credit card can be paid monthly, but even so, the longer it takes them to pay the amount borrowed in full, the more they have to pay. This is called an "interest," which is something that we have already covered in past chapters. However, there are other things that they must be aware of. One of those things is fees. They will be charged a late fee if they do not pay on time every month. If the late fee is not paid in full with the next monthly payment, another late fee will be incurred. If this goes on for too long the bank or financial institution that issued the card might even close their accounts, which does not necessarily eliminate what they owe to the bank; it will make it worse.

Then, there are the purchase limits that are usually imposed by the credit card issuer, which are the maximum amounts they can spend on the card. After reaching that limit, they will not be able to use the credit card anymore until part of the balance is paid off. However, they should refrain from maximizing their credit card since this will be hard to pay off. Billing statements issued by the credit card issuer allow you to know exactly how much you owe and the minimum amount you must pay monthly. The bank usually sends a billing statement every month, so you should alert them to stay on top of that. Nowadays, if their bank has online banking, this is usually sent through the bank app and email.

Now, onto the credit score and credit reporting. When it comes to borrowing money from a bank or any other financial institution, their reputation for being able to repay debts is essential for the acceptance of the loan, how much they can borrow, and even the interest rate they will pay on the borrowed money. The loan or credit card issuer will look into the borrower's history, any reports issued, and anything else involving their credit usage. When identifying the creditworthiness of an individual, banks and other lending institutions will look at their credit score. This way, they can quickly check if this person is trustworthy, and they can lend them money or issue a credit card. The higher the credit score, the more chances they have to be lent a higher amount (or increase their purchasing limits) and the better interest rate they can get. Any late payments or high credit usage will negatively impact the credit score, among many other things.

USING A CREDIT CARD RESPONSIBLY

Besides teaching your kid the basics of how to use a credit card and warning them about the interest and fees that credit cards might incur, there are other things that need to be discussed. For instance, you should talk to them about the benefits of responsible usage of a credit card beyond the problem of letting them accumulate a large amount of debt or using it senselessly. Using a credit card is okay when we understand what it can do for us in terms of our finances. This includes things like getting a better mortgage, a better interest rate on a car loan, or even having better deals with credit cards, such as more points, no-interest financing, cashback, and many other benefits.

The best way to test their knowledge before they start having credit cards and building debt is to allow them to use one of your credit cards. This way, you can get cashback every time they purchase something with your credit card, earn points, etc., but give them some of what you earn so they can understand. So, for instance, if after a few purchases with the credit card, they've got $10, you should either buy them something or give them $10 in cash so they can save. Allowing them to see the benefits physically will help them better understand the benefits of using a credit card responsibly.

Keeping the credit utilization ratio low is another way to use a credit card responsibly. This is because, besides allowing you to manage the debt better, the credit utilization ratio is a factor that credit score companies look into when calculating your credit score. It is important to note that this parameter is an average of all credit cards you have, so keeping all credit card utilization ratios low is important. Reading the credit statement every time you get a new one can help spot any errors that might occur. This is something that happens frequently, so teach your kid to go through every statement each month thoroughly. This is also a good time to check if any fraudulent charges have been made to your card. Choosing credit cards that suit your lifestyle is also a good idea. For instance, you need to know why you need a credit card; then, you can get the best card to maximize its benefits. If you fly often, having a credit card that gives you miles every time you make a purchase that can be exchanged for cheaper plane tickets might save you a lot of money. You should also avoid credit cards that have annual fees, especially with your first credit card. There are rare circumstances where paying an annual fee might be beneficial, but usually, these are not good for someone who is just starting out. Keeping your credit card account open even if you do not use it anymore can also improve your credit score because another parameter is the length of time you have had the account open. You do not have to use the credit card; if it does not have an annual fee, you should keep it. I didn't know about this when I was starting out with credit cards as a teenager. From age 18 to 22, I opened and closed five or six credit cards. It would have been better if I had just kept them all open.

THE IMPORTANCE OF A GOOD CREDIT SCORE

We've already seen some of the factors that might influence your credit score, like payment history or credit utilization. But there are many others that can make your credit score go up or down depending on how you use your credit card. For example, having a good credit mix where you have not only a credit card but also a mortgage or a car loan, and you're able to pay everything on time might increase your credit score. Also, the number of recent inquiries lenders have made into your credit history might also make a difference. Lenders might see this as a negative aspect if you have too many inquiries during a specific period.

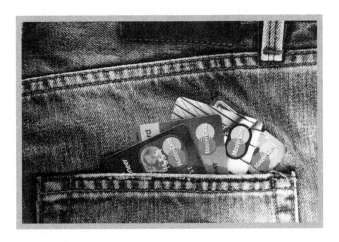

There's no magic number when it comes to credit scores, but because different credit score companies use different methods, you might have a good idea of what is considered a good credit score. For instance, if you have a credit score between 300 and 579, this is usually considered a very low score. Between 580 and 669 is considered fair but not great. The ranges between 670 and 739, as well as 740 and 799, are considered good and very good, respectively. Anything between 800 and 850 is considered excellent, so that's the range you want your credit score to fall into.

As I've said, having a good credit score can have many benefits, and we've also discussed some of them. A good or excellent credit score will allow you to get your credit approved much easier. Lenders are much more likely to approve any credit application you request, such as mortgages, personal loans, or credit cards. With a good credit score, these lenders will present you with much more attractive interest rates, which tend to be much lower than those of someone with a low or average credit score, and with this, also better loan terms. For example, you might get a lower fixed-rate mortgage, a higher credit limit on your credit card, or lower rates on car insurance. Speaking of credit cards, you might find that your credit card options become better with a higher credit score. This means that all the great credit cards with great bonuses and rewards will become available to you, which means you can save more money.

WHAT TO GO THROUGH WITH THEM ABOUT CREDIT

We've talked a lot about credit over this last chapter, but you have to have a solid plan to start talking about credit with your child so everything makes sense in their head. They will have to face credit at some point in their lives, so there's no time like now to get them involved with it and clearly explain what it is.

We've already established why credit is important, and they should know why it is by now. If they still don't get it, it's crucial that you make sure they do before moving forward. Remember, things like getting better credit cards that can help them save, getting low-interest loans, or getting better mortgages are all great benefits of having a good credit score. Credit scores are also something we went through, but we didn't really go deep into them, so I will explain the two main types of credit scores: FICO scores and VantageScore. FICO scores, which stands for Fair Isaac Corporation, is an entity often credited for the first credit score and is widely used to this day; it is also the one we've talked about the most in this book. These scores go from 300 to 850, containing five different categories when calculating the score.

While there's a more or less known weight percentage for each category, FICO states that these might change depending on the model's version of the score. So, for example, payment history is the category of credit score that weighs more in the FICO score, with around 35%. Payment history has to do with how often you make your payments on time. The total debt you have on credit cards, personal loans, etc., amounts to 30% of your FICO credit score. The length of credit history amounts to 15%, and it has to do with the length of time you've held a credit card, hence the importance of keeping your credit card account open even if you don't use the card. Then, 10% of the FICO credit score goes to the credit mix, which, as we've seen, is the amount of different credit you have, such as credit cards, mortgages, personal loans, or car loans. And lastly, 10% goes to new credit, so if you have a lot of new credit cards or credit in general created in a short period of time, this might have consequences for your credit score.

It's important to note that the FICO score also changes depending on the type of industry, so there is, for example, a FICO Bankcard Score or a FICO Auto Score that allows lenders to verify the creditworthiness of an applicant in a specific industry.

The VantageScore is a much newer model to calculate, and it takes data from the three major credit bureaus, unlike the FICO score. There are many different models of the VantageScore that use different formulas to calculate the credit score. For example, there's the VantageScore 4.0 and the 3.0 that use different percentages of the same categories, but the score is presented in a similar fashion to the FICO score from 300 to 850. While the percentages of the different categories are unknown, some categories influence the score more than others. For example, one of the very influential categories is credit utilization, so the more credit you've used overall, the lower your score will be. Then, below that in the influential category, you have the credit mix; below that is the payment history; and lastly, the least influential is the new credit acquired and the credit age. So, as you can see, the categories weigh differently in the different types of scores. Other types of credit score models are used, but they are not as popular as the two we've discussed above. Most of these alternative credit scores are custom credit score models.

The three major credit bureaus are Experian, TransUnion, and Equifax, and the information these three entities have on you forms your credit score through credit reports. So, what type of information is in a credit report? To start with, every one of the three credit bureaus has slightly different information about you, but there are usually four different categories they all have that might affect your credit score. This includes inquiries, public records, personal information, and credit accounts.

In the personal information category, you can find pretty standard information such as your name, date of birth, previous and current addresses, phone numbers, social security number, as well as past and current employment information. In the public records, you can find information that has been reported to a public entity that might have a negative impact on your report and credit score, such as tax liens, civil suits, bankruptcies, court judgments, foreclosures, or even overdue child support. However, these stay in your records for different amounts of time; for instance, foreclosures might remain in your records for ten years, but a Chapter 13 bankruptcy will only stay in your records for about seven years.

In the credit accounts category of the credit report, you will find information about your credit repayment history and total amounts borrowed. This includes things like mortgages, student loans, car loans, all your current and previous credit cards, etc. It will also have more details about the different credit accounts, such as the loan amount or credit limit, the date the account was opened or closed, the payment history for each account, the type of account, the account balance, and the name of the lender. Lastly, in the credit reports are the inquiries. Here, you can find two types of inquiries: hard and soft inquiries, but only the hard inquiries will affect your credit score. Hard inquiries happen when a lender checks your credit score or you've applied for a loan. Usually, these appear on your credit report for two years before disappearing. Soft inquiries don't affect your credit score and might happen when you check your own credit score, apply for a job where they check your background, or ask for a quote from an insurance company.

BUILDING CREDIT

There's a lot of talk about building credit, and your child will probably hear a lot of it through the years, and some of it will simply be false. You need to be the one who guides them through what is real and what is not. As a young adult, building credit might be confusing for them, but let's look at some of the most important things to do to build credit.

Having credit accounts can indeed help them build credit, as long as the bank or the lender reports this account to any of the credit bureaus and they use it responsibly. It is also true that building credit takes some time, and just because they've opened a credit card account and have been using it responsibly doesn't mean their credit score will shoot up in one day. The best way is to pay at least the minimum payment every month and make sure the payments are on time.

They have to be responsible when it comes to the use of credit. This is vital for them to understand because while it's hard to build up credit, it's pretty easy to lower it. The first thing you need to tell them when they get a credit card is to fully understand the account terms. This way, they will be prepared for any fees, interest, or due dates related to the credit they have and won't be caught by surprise. Staying way below the credit limit, and as I've said, staying below 30% is the best way to positively affect your credit score.

MONITORING ACCOUNTS

It's important to monitor the different credit accounts they have. We've seen that it's quite easy nowadays to check your bank account through your online banking app and even check the monthly statements. But monitoring your credit reports is also something you should do regularly. By going to Annual-CreditReport.com, you can check all the credit reports from the three major credit bureaus and look out for any mistakes that might have lowered your credit score or any other changes that might have affected it. Also, check your credit score since this doesn't appear in your credit reports, but you can check it through your account. You can also get your credit score from one of the three credit bureaus by going directly to them.

However, my preferred method is to use the free app Credit Karma. It is fast, easy and free, but they will try to get you to sign up for new credit cards or other accounts. I ignore all of those offerings in the app and use it to monitor my credit score and account activity.

GETTING THEM STARTED

Opening a checking and savings account is an excellent way for your kid to start building a good credit score. If they get a job, then even better; they will have their own money and, more importantly, they will understand the value of money. But there are other things that you can do to help them build a great credit score for the future.

One of these things is adding them as users on your own credit card. If you've been using your credit card properly, this shouldn't be a problem, and it's a great way to get your kid started and help them get a great credit score in the future. Even if they are simply authorized users of your credit card, they will receive their own card linked to your account, and besides appearing in your credit reports, this card will also appear on theirs. As authorized users, they can make purchases anywhere, but you are the only one who can make payments to the card. But make sure they pay for what they've spent, too, at the end of the month so that they start learning how it works. Alternatively, you can also add them as authorized users of the card but without access to your account, so this means that their credit can go up, but they are not allowed to purchase things that they will not be able to pay. This is a great method if you don't think your kid has the maturity to have access to your credit card account. You have to create rules either way, so they know how much they can use and how they should pay for the credit they've used.

When it's time for your kid to go to college, please encourage them to apply for a student credit card. At this point, if you taught them well, they should have great money habits, so they might be able to apply for their first credit card on their own. These student credit cards usually have higher interest rates but much lower credit limits than regular credit cards, but it will definitely be a good experience for them. If they are under the age of 21, they will have to prove that they have some sort of income, so a part-time job would be ideal if they want to get a student credit card. However, you can also become a cosigner, which makes you responsible for managing the account. Alternatively, suppose they can't get a student credit card for whatever reason. In that case, they can still apply for a different credit card, usually a secured credit card, where they might have to pay a deposit that is the same as the credit limit the credit card will have. However, many of these types of cards come with hefty fees, but if they are able to pay for what they spend every month, that shouldn't be a problem.

Building good credit is fundamental; the earlier they start, the more established their credit score will be once they grow up. The first step is teaching them about credit cards and using them responsibly. Then, you can move on to what a credit score is and why it is essential to have a good one. Talk about all the different parameters credit bureaus use to calculate the credit score, such as length of credit history, credit mix, recent inquiries, payment history, and credit utilization, as well as all the benefits that come with having a great credit score, such as lower interest rates, better loan terms, etc. Then, you can move on to what credit really is and how they can build a good credit score, but you will need to help them if you want them to start early. Allow them to be an authorized user of your credit card, or encourage them to take out a student credit card or a secured credit card.

CONCLUSION

You now have all the essential information you need to teach your kid how to become financially literate and lead a stable and prosperous life regarding their finances. It's a long journey, but one that is worth walking because, after all, it is our children we are talking about, and we want nothing but the best for them. When introducing them to the finance world and the economy, the first thing you need to talk to them about (assuming they are kids and have no experience with any of that side of the world) is what money is. Money, whether we like it or not, moves the world around and is an essential piece of our society. It is a tool that allows us to purchase things such as food or a house or pay for services such as energy, streaming TV, and everything else we need to live and survive. This concept of money might be a little strange for your kid if they are young, but you need to start slowly by first showing them the different denominations of coins and bills and what each one is worth. Then, when they can differentiate between the various bills and coins, you need to introduce them to a more abstract concept: the value of money. Even if your kid knows all the coins and bills and knows precisely how much each is worth, the concept of money's value is different. Usually, they have no idea of the concept of money. They are probably used to you buying everything just by swiping a card or taking a banknote out of your wallet. The education system provides some basic information to our children, but it comes down to us to teach them efficient ways of preparing them for their future.

This is where the journey of teaching your kid to become financially literate starts, and the younger you start teaching them about it, the easier it will be for them to develop good money habits and the better they will understand the financial world. The more you discuss the purpose of money, the more they will get comfortable with the topic, and it will no longer be this ugly monster that many kids (and adults) seem to think it is. You need to make it fun and allow them to interact, or they will lose interest. One enjoyable activity, as previously discussed, is to accompany them shopping and show them how to pay for items. Seeing what is happening and how transactions are made makes a lot more sense to them than simply explaining the concepts to them. However, along with the teaching and the interactive part of learning, you must be a financial example for them. You can't teach them something and then do the opposite. Kids tend to copy things from their parents, and they are incredibly observant. So, whenever you are with them (and even when you're alone), you should try to set a good example by doing the things that you taught them. Allowing them to handle money is also part of the interactive part that you should aim to incorporate. This means allowing them to grab a few coins and bills, or even your debit card, and letting them make the payment so they have a feel for the real thing. Once they grow a little older, you should let them shop for themselves, but always with a list of the things they need to buy and the exact amount of money so they don't deviate from the things they need to purchase. If they throw a tantrum and want to buy something else they've seen in a store, you can allow them, but then there will be no more money for the things they need. This will teach them the lesson of perseverance and not getting distracted from their goals.

At the beginning of this journey, it will also be hard for us parents to control ourselves in certain circumstances. There are also a few "rules" that you need to remember, such as avoiding the subject of finances completely or postponing it as much as you can is never a good solution. In the same vein, assuming that they will learn by themselves is simply wrong because they will make all the mistakes before they can learn anything. Many parents assume they are too young to get into those concepts and postpone the subject, but we often underestimate our kids, which is something we shouldn't do. Another big mistake we parents tend to make is managing all the important decisions for our children. If you keep on doing this, they will never learn, no matter how much you explain everything to them. They actually need to do things themselves and go through the process.

However, you also have to remember what your child's age is. If they are toddlers or preschoolers, you must teach them the basics before moving on to different subjects. If you follow this book, everything is written from the most basic of the concepts to the more complex ones, and it's a great way to teach them about being financially literate. Once they know the basics and are a little older and able to move on from those basics, you need to introduce them to goal setting. This is a crucial part of learning how to live a stable life financially. Teaching them about the most common mistakes people make is also vital, and this can include a lack of goals, living on borrowed money, using credit cards for everyday payments, or spending without limits.

Once they are old enough to work a part-time job, you should encourage them to do so. But before that, when they are young, you need to introduce them to the concept of work. Why do we work, and how do we get money from working? However, you have to tell them that we not only work for money; there are many other benefits that someone can get from going to work. I've listed many different things teenagers can do to start making money from work, but you need to help them find what they are happy doing. Allow them to experiment and choose what makes them happy because they will carry this feeling into their adult lives later. Whatever they choose at this age, you should encourage them no matter what.

Spending is part of life, but we can choose to spend senselessly, or we can choose to spend wisely, and that's the lesson we need to teach them. The concept of delayed gratification is a great one to start with by developing their self-control and encouraging them to wait for the things that really matter. Controlling their impulse buying is another way to teach them how to spend wisely. For this, you need to teach them how to create and follow a budget, make a shopping list every time they go out to purchase something, learn how to control their emotions and use the waiting period technique before buying something they think they want. When budgeting, tracking expenses is fundamental. I've detailed many ways you can teach them how to do it, but perhaps the more straightforward way is to use a budgeting app for kids so they can have an interactive and fun way to control their budget and see their money grow.

Saving is also something that they should be familiar with. Tell them the main reason why we should save and the different ways they can save. Set short-, medium-, and long-term goals so they can have an incentive and get them to use an app to track their savings and know how far they are from accomplishing their financial goals. By this time, you should introduce them to bank accounts by opening a savings account and potentially a checking account as well. This is a safe way for them to keep their money and allow it to grow over time.

Once they reach their teenage years, it's time to introduce them to investing. This is a practice that takes time for them to get used to and learn enough about to invest their money confidently. It's vital that you make it simple at first so they get motivated to learn more. Again, opening a brokerage account and having some money there for them to give it a try is ideal to keep them motivated. If that's not yet a possibility, invest some of their money in your brokerage account and allow them to check in once in a while. Investing is a vast subject, so you might have to go through the concept of due diligence a few times, practice with them, and teach them the different investment vehicles they can use.

Borrowing money and building good credit are also concepts for older kids who already have a good understanding of finances and the economy. Allowing them to have a credit card might be a good idea if you think they are responsible enough, as long as they pay it off quickly with their own money. Explain to them the consequences of allowing a credit card debt to grow while also teaching them the benefits of it, such as the ability to establish good credit by using the card. It's also important to teach them the methods for getting out of debt in case they get into one. There are many things they can do to pay off debt quickly, and even though you might not want to think about your child getting into crippling debt, it's better that they know the methods to get out of it before it's too late.

As you can see, there's a lot to teach, but being financially literate in today's world is extremely important. Whatever you do, make sure they have fun while learning and that they create good money habits as they grow so they can bring that into their adult lives and live a financially stress-free life.

I hope you've enjoyed your journey through "Teaching Kids Good Money Habits" as much as I enjoyed creating it for you. Your commitment to shaping young minds and instilling wise financial habits is truly commendable.

As you reflect on the valuable insights you've gained, I kindly request a small favor that can make a big difference. Could you spare a moment to share your thoughts about the book? Your honest review will provide me with valuable feedback and help other parents, caregivers, and educators discover the book's benefits.

Leaving a review is simple:

Scan the QR code to the left to leave a review on Amazon.

Share your thoughts and rate the book.

Click "Submit," and you're done!

Thank you for being a part of our mission to empower the next generation with solid money skills. Your review is a gift that keeps on giving.

Scan this QR code to visit the MarVas Publishing website. You can see all of our books, send us a message or join our mailing list to get notified about future books.

ABOUT THE AUTHOR

Mario A. Vasquez is a dynamic 45-year-old author whose expertise lies in the realms of Personal Finance, Corporate Finance, and Business Strategies.

With an impressive background in finance and a track record of successful ventures, Mario is driven by a relentless passion for empowering individuals and businesses to achieve financial mastery. His journey began as a financial analyst, where he honed his skills working for top-tier financial executives.

Mario's dedication to demystifying complex financial concepts led him to put pen to paper. His writing embodies his commitment to providing practical and actionable advice to readers at all levels of financial literacy. Through his meticulously crafted books, he breaks down intricate financial strategies into easily digestible insights, making the world of finance accessible to both novices and seasoned professionals.

Beyond his role as an accomplished author, Mario is a sought-after speaker at international finance conferences and webinars, where his charismatic delivery and profound knowledge captivate audiences. His mission is to shift the paradigm of financial decision-making, arming individuals and businesses with the tools they need to secure their financial futures.

In an era where financial literacy is paramount, Mario's books have become invaluable companions for those navigating the complexities of personal and corporate finance. His dynamic approach, unwavering dedication, and contagious enthusiasm have made him a respected authority and a relentless advocate for sound financial practices. Through his work, Mario A. Vasquez is reshaping the finance landscape, one page at a time.

Join the conversation about finance and business with Mario by emailing MarVasPublishing@gmail.com. Your inquiries and thoughts are always welcome as we work together toward financial excellence.

GLOSSARY

Asset: something that has value and that someone or a company can own. This can be cash, shares, or property.

Annual Percentage Rate (APR): This is the interest rate charged for money borrowed or earned on investments in a year.

Automated Teller Machine (ATM): a terminal where, by introducing a debit card, one can have access to their account and withdraw money, make payments, or check their balance

Bank: a financial institution that offers money services such as loans or a place where someone can stash their money

Brokerage Account: an account that allows you to invest in the stock market and other financial vehicles and also allows you to keep money

Budget: This is a plan that should be made when someone

wants to plan their spending, whether it is daily, weekly, monthly, or annually.

Checking Account: a bank account that people use to keep their money and typically comes with a debit card and physical checks as a way to spend or get access to their money.

Credit: a deal where someone or a company provides money that can be paid later on with interest.

Credit Card: a bank card that allows us to purchase goods or services on credit, using the bank's money. This money has to be paid later, typically with interest applied.

Credit Score: a score that lets people know how creditworthy they are and helps lenders understand the likelihood of the person repaying the borrowed money.

Debit Card: a bank card that allows us to pay for things with money from their own account linked to it, typically a checking account.

Debt: money that we owe to someone or a company.

Emergency Fund: money people set aside to pay for things in case of an emergency or something unexpected happens.

Financial Literacy: the knowledge one has to manage their financial resources and make sound financial decisions.

Fixed Expenses: bills that are due in regular intervals, typically monthly. Examples include rent, mortgage, car payment, cell phone bill, electricity and other loan payments, just to name a phew.

Income: money that someone earns through employment or investments.

Interest Rate: the percentage of the money charged to someone for borrowing said money. This is typically shown as an annual number but can be calculated or discussed in other lengths, such as monthly.

Profit: the difference between expenses and revenue when this is positive. If negative, it is a loss instead of a profit.

Savings: the method of setting aside money to spend it later, typically with a goal of growing in value.

Tax: a fee issued by the government on someone or on a business that has income.

REFERENCES

Adams, R., & CPA. (2022, January 24). *How to invest as a teenager or minor [start under 18 years old]*. Young and Invested. https://youngandtheinvested.com/how-to-invest-as-teenager/

Akalp, N. (2014, June 17). *How to help your kids launch a small business this summer*. Forbes. https://www.forbes.com/sites/allbusiness/2014/06/17/how-to-help-your-kids-launch-a-small-business-this-summer/?sh=4cd2e41e6aeb

Akalp, N. (2016, June 9). *6 ways to help your kid start a business and learn about life*. Entrepreneur. https://www.entrepreneur.com/leadership/6-ways-to-help-your-kid-start-a-business-and-learn-about/276753

Andreevska, D. (2017, June 3). *How can you teach your kids about real estate investing?* Investment Property Tips | Mashvisor Real Estate Blog. https://www.mashvisor.com/blog/teach-kids-real-estate-investing/

The Ascent Staff. (2019, August 27). *The 8 cardinal rules of using a credit card*. The Motley Fool. https://www.fool.com/the-ascent/credit-cards/articles/the-8-cardinal-rules-of-using-a-credit-card/

Bankaroo. (n.d.). *Money goals for kids of different ages – bankaroo* :: Virtual bank for kids. Bankaroo. https://www.bankaroo.com/money-goals-for-kids-of-different-ages/

Bankaroo Team. (n.d.). *5 things your child must understand about debt*. Bankaroo. https://www.bankaroo.com/5-things-your-child-must-understand-about-debt/

Beattie, A. (2021, December 28). *How to teach your child about investing*. Investopedia. https://www.investopedia.com/articles/pf/07/childinvestor.asp

Brown, L. (2021, April 11). *How to spend less on meals at home* | the straits times. Straitstimes. https://www.straitstimes.com/business/invest/how-to-spend-less-on-meals-at-home

Burnette, M. (2022, July 15). *4 smart ways to teach kids about saving money*. NerdWallet. https://www.nerdwallet.com/article/banking/4-smart-ways-to-teach-kids-about-saving-money

Caldwell, M. (2021, December 30). *The 10 biggest money mistakes you can make.* The Balance. https://www.thebalancemoney.com/biggest-money-mistakes-2385535

Capital One Team. (2022, May 12). *6 lessons to teach credit to your kids and teens.* Capital One. https://www.capitalone.com/learn-grow/money-management/teaching-kids-about-credit/

Cohen, J. (n.d.). *5 tips on how to explain debt to children* | lemonade day. Lemonadeday. https://lemonadeday.org/blog/5-tips-how-explain-debt-children

Colestock, S. (2022, November 22). *Best money and budgeting apps for kids, teens and young adults.* The Dough Roller. https://www.doughroller.net/personal-finance/budgeting/best-money-apps-for-kids-teens-and-young-adults/

Cruze, R. (2021, December 14). *Impulse buying: Why we do it and how to stop.* Ramsey Solutions. https://www.ramseysolutions.com/budgeting/stop-impulse-buys

Davies, M. (2022, August 8). *42% were denied financial products due to credit scores.* LendingTree. https://www.lendingtree.com/personal/credit-scores-financial-products-survey/

Doyle, G. (2020, January 21). *Do not save what is left after spending; instead spend what is left after saving.* RBC Wealth Management. https://ca.rbcwealthmanagement.com/gerry.doyle/blog/2303780-Do-not-save-what-is-left-after-spending-instead-spend-what-is-left-after-saving----Warren-Buffett/

Edmond, N. (2022, March 7). *10 mistakes parents make when teaching kids about money.* MoneyTime SA. https://moneytimekids.co.za/blogs/news/10-mistakes-parents-make-when-teaching-kids-about-money

Edwards, S. (2018, January 23). *5 benefits of teaching young children about entrepreneurship.* Entrepreneur. https://www.entrepreneur.com/leadership/5-benefits-of-teaching-young-children-about-entrepreneurship/292631

Fergunson, D. (2021, December 13). *How to teach children the real value of money.* The Guardian. https://www.theguardian.com/money/2021/dec/13/how-to-teach-children-the-real-value-of-money

Forbes. (n.d.). *Forbes quotes.* Forbes. https://www.forbes.com/quotes/496/

FSB. (n.d.). *3 reasons why you should have a savings account* | FSB blog. Fsb1879. https://www.fsb1879.com/blog/3-reasons-why-people-should-have-savings-accounts

Garcia, N. (2022, October 19). *How to explain to your kids why you work.* Sleeping Should Be Easy. https://sleepingshouldbeeasy.com/why-you-work/

George, D. (2020, January 4). *It's not always how much money you earn, it's how you use it.* Fool. https://www.fool.com/the-ascent/buying-stocks/articles/its-not-always-how-much-money-you-earn-its-how-you-use-it/

Gran, B. (2023, January 18). *Get your children saving: A guide to kids' savings accounts* – Forbes advisor. Forbes. https://www.forbes.com/advisor/banking/savings/guide-to-childrens-and-kids-savings-accounts/

Hines, C. M. (2017, November 26). *10 money lessons to help your kids avoid debt.* KC Parent Magazine. https://kcparent.com/parenting/10-money-lessons-to-help-your-kids-avoid-debt/

Independent Observer Team. (2022, April 18). *Debt is like any other trap, easy enough to get into, but hard enough to get out of.* OBSERVER. https://observerid.com/debt-is-like-any-other-trap-easy-enough-to-get-into-but-hard-enough-to-get-out-of-josh-billings/#:~:text=%E2%80%9CDebt%20is%20like%20any%20other

Irby, L. (2022, June 7). *Tips for teaching your child about using a credit card.* The Balance. https://www.thebalancemoney.com/teach-your-child-about-credit-cards-960193

Kagan, J. (2018). *Savings account.* Investopedia. https://www.investopedia.com/terms/s/savingsaccount.asp

Karr, A. (2023, January 17). *Why it's important to save money at an early age.* Mydoh. https://www.mydoh.ca/learn/money-101/money-basics/why-kids-and-teens-should-start-saving-money-early/

Kramer, P. (2005, October 5). *Teaching kids the value of money.* Parents; Parents. https://www.parents.com/parenting/money/family-finances/teaching-kids-value-of-money/

Loiacono, S. (2021, January 12). *Rules that Warren Buffett lives by.* Investopedia. https://www.investopedia.com/financial-edge/0210/rules-that-warren-buffett-lives-by.aspx

Musalia, W. (2022, August 2). *Delaying gratification: Why waiting a little longer pays more.* Money254. https://www.money254.co.ke/post/delaying-gratification-why-waiting-a-little-longer-pays-more-money-management

My Doh Team. (2022, September 19). *Types of debt and their meaning.* Mydoh.

https://www.mydoh.ca/learn/money-101/debt/types-of-debt-and-their-meaning/

Mydoh. (2021, January 20). *How to budget for kids.* Mydoh. https://www.mydoh.ca/learn/money-101/money-basics/how-to-create-a-budget-for-kids-and-teens/

MyDoh Team. (2022, September 18). *How to pay off debt fast: a guide for parents and teens.* Mydoh. https://www.mydoh.ca/learn/money-101/debt/how-to-pay-off-debt-fast-a-guide-for-parents-and-teens/

Norris, E. (2022, June 14). *Top 10 most common financial mistakes.* Investopedia. https://www.investopedia.com/personal-finance/most-common-financial-mistakes/

PSN Team. (n.d.). *10 tips for teaching kids to spend less!* – parenting special needs magazine. Parenting Special Needs. https://www.parentingspecialneeds.org/article/10-tips-for-teaching-kids-to-spend-less/

R, D. (2019, May 12). *The importance of goal setting for children.* ChildWatch. https://childwatch.com/blog/2019/05/11/the-importance-of-goal-setting-for-children/

Ramsey Solutions. (2022, July 8). *How to balance your checking account.* Ramsey Solutions. https://www.ramseysolutions.com/banking/how-to-balance-your-checking-account

Reader's Digest Editors. (2022, September 8). *7 ways to teach your children about money* - reader's digest. Www.readersdigest.co.uk. https://www.readersdigest.co.uk/money/managing-your-money/7-ways-to-teach-your-children-about-money

Ruth, A. (2015, July 21). *Robert Kiyosaki - it isn't about how much you make.* Due. https://due.com/blog/robert-kiyosaki-it-isnt-about-how-much-you-make/

Ryan. (2020, October 21). *Goal setting for kids | importance & motivational examples.* ID Tech. https://www.idtech.com/blog/goal-setting-for-kids-importance-motivational-examples

Ryan Webber, M. (2022, December 25). *How to open a CD for a child.* Investopedia. https://www.investopedia.com/how-to-open-a-cd-for-a-child-5248856

Schwahn, L. (2021, October 25). *11 ways to make money as a kid for any age.* Nerd-Wallet. https://www.nerdwallet.com/article/finance/make-money-as-a-kid

Sharna, K. (2022, March 25). *How to help your child find their passion | The Asian School*. The Asian School. https://www.theasianschool.net/blog/how-to-help-your-child-find-their-passion/#0-here-know-the-ways-how-to-help-your-child-find-their-passion

Spero Financial. (2019, February 12). *9 mistakes parents make when teaching kids about money*. Spero Financial. https://spero.financial/9-mistakes-parents-make-when-teaching-kids-about-money/

Tretina, K., & Schimdt, J. (2022, January 20). *Investing for kids: Give the gift of stock* – Forbes Advisor. Forbes. https://www.forbes.com/advisor/investing/investing-for-kids-stock/

Ulzheimer, J. (2023, February 23). *How many Americans have bad credit?* BadCredit.org. https://www.badcredit.org/how-to/how-many-americans-have-bad-credit/

Vamdatt, R. (2020a, March 24). *What is money? A simple definition for kids, teens and beginners*. Easy Peasy Finance for Kids and Beginners. https://www.easypeasyfinance.com/money-for-kids-teens-financial-literacy/

Vamdatt, R. (2020b, October 30). *What is investing? A simple explanation for kids, teens & beginners*. Easy Peasy Finance for Kids and Beginners. https://www.easypeasyfinance.com/investing-for-kids-financial-literacy/

Winter, D. (2022, October 4). *Kid-powered businesses: 12 ideas for future ceos*. Shopify. https://www.shopify.com/blog/business-ideas-for-kids

Young, K. (2018, November 30). *5 ways to teach kids how to save at home | America Saves*. Americasaves. https://americasaves.org/resource-center/insights/5-ways-to-teach-kids-how-to-save-at-home/

IMAGE REFERENCES

Akyurt, E. (2018). *Black and white dartboard*. In Pexels. https://www.pexels.com/photo/black-and-white-dartboard-1552617/

Barbhuiya, T. (2022). *Woman paying in a store with her credit card*. [images] In Pexels. https://www.pexels.com/photo/woman-paying-in-a-store-with-her-credit-card-11412587/

Cup of Couple. (2021). *A man with an afro hair holding a credit card*. [images] In

Pexels. https://www.pexels.com/photo/a-man-with-an-afro-hair-holding-a-credit-card-6956772/

energepic. (2016). *Close-up photo of monitor.* [images] In Pexels. https://www.pexels.com/photo/close-up-photo-of-monitor-159888/

Expect Best. (2017). *Buildings with glass windows.* [images] In Pexels. https://www.pexels.com/photo/buildings-with-glass-windows-351264/

Fairytale, E. (2020). *Photo of woman cooking near her family.* [images] In Pexels. https://www.pexels.com/photo/photo-of-woman-cooking-near-her-family-3807332/

Fring, G. (2020). *Woman with shopping bags sitting on chair.* [images] In Pexels. https://www.pexels.com/photo/woman-with-shopping-bags-sitting-on-chair-5622847/

Grabowska, K. (2020a). *Composition of calculator with paper money and notebook with pen.* [images] In Pexels. https://www.pexels.com/photo/composition-of-calculator-with-paper-money-and-notebook-with-pen-4386341/

Grabowska, K. (2020b). *Crop man counting dollar banknotes.* [images] In Pexels. https://www.pexels.com/photo/crop-man-counting-dollar-banknotes-4386431/

Grabowska, K. (2020c). *Crop person showing twenty dollar bill and miniature USA flag.* [images] In Pexels. https://www.pexels.com/photo/crop-person-showing-twenty-dollar-bill-and-miniature-usa-flag-4386447/

Grabowska, K. (2020d). *Heap of money on white surface.* [images] In Pexels. https://www.pexels.com/photo/heap-of-money-on-white-surface-4386473/

Piacquadio, A. (2020a). *Woman working as a cashier.* [images] In Pexels. https://www.pexels.com/photo/woman-working-as-a-cashier-3801439/

Piacquadio, A. (2020b). *Content woman using laptop in street cafe.* [images] In Pexels. https://www.pexels.com/photo/content-woman-using-laptop-in-street-cafe-3808128/

Pixabay. (2016a). *Person holding debit card.* [images] In Pexels. https://www.pexels.com/photo/shopping-business-money-pay-50987/

Pixabay. (2016b). *Black calculator near ballpoint pen on white printed paper.* [images] In Pexels. https://www.pexels.com/photo/black-calculator-near-ballpoint-pen-on-white-printed-paper-53621/

Pixabay. (2016c). *Blue master card on denim pocket.* [images] In Pexels.

https://www.pexels.com/photo/blue-master-card-on-denim-pocket-164571/

Pixabay. (2017). *Numbers on monitor.* [images] In Pexels. https://www.pexels.com/photo/airport-bank-board-business-534216/

rimthong, maitree. (2018). *Person putting coin in a piggy bank.* [images] In Pexels. https://www.pexels.com/photo/person-putting-coin-in-a-piggy-bank-1602726/

Subiyanto, K. (2020). *Kids making noise and disturbing mom working at home.* [images] In Pexels. https://www.pexels.com/photo/kids-making-noise-and-disturbing-mom-working-at-home-4474035/

ThisIsEngineering. (2020). *Person holding black tablet.* [images] In Pexels. https://www.pexels.com/photo/person-holding-black-tablet-3912956/

Printed in Great Britain
by Amazon

41517181R00086